2003
CODING
WORKBOOK
for the Physician's Office

Alice Covell, CMA-A, RMA, CPC

THOMSON

DELMAR LEARNING

Australia Canada Mexico Singapore Spain United Kingdom United States

THOMSON
DELMAR LEARNING

2003 Coding Workbook for the Physician's Office
by Alice G. Covell

Vice President, Health Care Business Unit:
William Brottmiller

Editorial Director:
Cathy L. Esperti

Acquisitions Editor:
Rhonda Dearborn

Developmental Editor:
Marjorie A. Bruce

Marketing Director:
Jennifer McAvey

Marketing Coordinator:
Mona Caron

Editorial Assistant:
Natalie Wager

Production Director:
Karen Leet

Production Editor:
James Zayicek

Library of Congress Cataloging-in-Publication Data

ISBN 1-4018-5210-6

Notice to the Reader

Contents

Preface

Many billers learn to code on their own, by trial and error. They open the books, search for a code, and take the first one that looks correct. If they use an inaccurate code on a medical claim form, the payer may reject or pay incorrectly for that service. Insurance companies monitor the reported procedures and diagnoses, looking for fraud or abuse. Medicare, HMOs, the Blues, and other payers issue utilization reports advising physicians that their reported services differ from those of their peers. These reports can be the precursor for audit by that payer. These are money matters but coding can impact medical issues. Disease registries state that patients are enrolled for care with an erroneous diagnosis. As a result, the doctor receives information on treatment of the wrong medical condition.

With so much of medicine and patient care decided by these codes, why is it so difficult to get them right? Most physicians do not speak code, at least not fluently. The terms in the coding references are concise, developed by a committee that carefully chooses which words to use. Busy doctors and other professionals describe their services in their own way. This becomes a bigger problem when English is the doctor's second language. Also, there are changes in procedure and diagnosis codes every year. Many office documents and computer systems contain obsolete codes.

Hospitals code differently than medical offices. Facilities may use CPT® for coding some outpatient services, but hospitals do not perform medical visits or surgery. Those are physician services. Unlike hospitals, insurers pay doctors on a fee for service basis. The doctor performs a service, bills it, and the payer sends a check. Both hospitals and doctors use the same diagnosis reference, ICD-9-CM, but the doctor's office may be limited to reporting only one code, the "best" one for the service. The U. S. Department of Health and Human Services (DHHS) developed official guidelines for coding diagnoses. Most of the guidelines apply to hospital reporting. Only sixteen rules specify diagnosis reporting by physicians. These instructions for physician coding appear later in this workbook.

Now that you have had the bad news, here is the good news. None of the coding process is secret. There are no hidden rules in obscure volumes. To master coding, all you do is read and think. Coding is logical, and it can be fun. So settle down with your coding references and this workbook, and enjoy.

Alice Covell, CMA-A, RMA, CPC

Coding and Medical Insurance Policies

Coding can be significant in receiving, and keeping, payment for medical services. One publication says that coding makes a 25% greater or lesser difference in payment. It is the insurance policy language that defines payable benefits. Beginning coders may ask, "What code do I use to get paid?" A patient, not receiving payment, may say that the doctor reported the "wrong" code. The answer for both situations is clear. You always use the correct code.

Doctors find coding confusing. They may do a new service that does not have a specific code. Do we report it with an existing code number? Sometimes the procedure is not really new, but the doctor uses a new technique or technology. Medicare, the Blues, or another payer may notify the doctors to report these services under another code. However, without specific instructions to call the service something different, you should report it under the "unlisted procedure" code. The "Instructions for Use of the CPT Book" emphasize this point by stating, "Do not select a CPT code that merely approximates the service provided. If no such procedure exists, then report the service using the appropriate unlisted procedure or service code." The insurer can decide to pay or reject the claim, based on the policy coverage.

Perhaps a new code is now available for a recently developed procedure. Unfortunately, the service may be too new to appear on the insurance policy benefit list and so the payer rejects the claim. The doctor now wonders if you should code it with last year's code. You may decide to make the change after offering explanations to the irate patient who now has a large, unexpected bill. In these no-win situations, it may seem easier to recode and rebill the service. Don't do it. Resist that temptation. The medical record does not support any code but the correct one.

Insurers match the claims with their benefit schedule. Medicare pays for only a few preventive services. Religious organizations may have policies that do not cover sterilizations or abortions. Payers then send the doctor or policyholder the specified payment or a rejection. If you change the code to make the service payable, it is fraud. Also, a service may not be payable for the given diagnosis. Suppose the doctor sees a patient for bronchitis and notices that it is time to repeat the electrocardiogram as the patient has a family history of heart disease. If the office bills the ECG with the diagnosis of bronchitis, the payer probably will reject the service. Taking an ECG is not a standard procedure for bronchitis. It is correct to report the office visit for bronchitis and the family history of heart disease for the ECG.

Some situations are less clear. No insurer would deny a person the reconstruction of their nose following a serious auto accident, a fall from a horse, or similar incident. What if the injury occurred ten years ago? Should the auto insurer, the owner of the stable or the patient's own insurance pay the doctor's bill? Is the patient's health insurance primary, and expected to pay first before the other insurers? All these health insurance payment problems do not affect the determination of the correct diagnosis and procedure codes.

Medicare and private insurance are separate programs. Medicare's coding rules work and the Health Insurance Portability and Accountability Act (HIPAA) is requiring insurers to adopt the government approved coding specifications of Medicare and Medicaid. If you work for a pediatrician, becoming aware of Medicare rules may be difficult. Pay close attention to payer bulletins and the information on coding distributed at their seminars and workshops. Many private organizations and medical specialty societies offer coding workshops. Try to attend one each year, and always end the year with the purchase of new coding references.

Conquering Coding

You may be surprised how much experience you have with coding. You use it every day. From social security, telephone, and credit card numbers, to thermometers and cable television selectors, numbers that represent words surround us. If you see $1.00, you think "one dollar." Even without a description or explanation, you probably recognize 1-800-555-1212.

Our present diagnosis coding system is ICD-9-CM, the International Classification of Diseases, Ninth Revision, Clinical Modification. Disease coding systems began in the late 1800s and identified the causes of death. The ICD system is now used worldwide to record the incidence of disease. Many ICD-9-CM reference books include this history. Take the time to read this fascinating summary of disease recording. ICD-9-CM is a three-volume reference, available from many sources at prices ranging from $19.95 to almost $200.00.

The American Medical Association (AMA) developed the procedure, or service coding reference, Current Procedural Terminology, or CPT®. This single volume reference is available from many sources, but the AMA carefully protects the copyright and printing of CPT.

The Health Care Financing Administration (HCFA), now named the Centers for Medicare and Medicaid Services (CMS), the agency responsible for Medicare and Medicaid, recognized that many medical services were not physician services. To report, pay, and monitor ambulance services, medical equipment and supplies, another set of codes was needed. This system is now called the Healthcare Common Procedure Coding System (formerly the HCFA Common Procedure Coding System), or HCPCS (pronounced "hick-picks"). HCPCS has three levels of codes, usually indicated by Roman numerals. The Level I codes are the CPT codes, five digit, all numeric codes. Level II codes have a letter followed by four numbers. The Level III codes are "local" codes, beginning with W, X, Y or Z. Level III codes, if acceptable at all, are defined and supplied by your local Medicare or Medicaid carrier. X1234 may represent a different service in Montana, Missouri and Maine. Few payers other than Medicare or Medicaid will accept Level III codes and HIPAA will eventually eliminate the Level III codes.

Coding determines the appropriateness of treatment and the medical necessity for a service. Insurers compile statistics on the frequency of a service, sometimes identifying "abused" procedures. They state that many doctors do C-sections for their own convenience rather than patient need. Monitoring the codes billed, Michigan Blue Shield found a physician who did almost half the endoscopic procedures reported in one year. A Medicaid program discovered a doctor who reported over 400 house calls in one day. The payers, like you, found these data unbelievable, audited the physicians, and recovered the overpayments.

Coding Ground Rules

I.   Keep your coding references current. Purchase new books each year.

II. Know the coding rules and apply them properly.

III. Code only what the documentation supports.

IV. Match the diagnosis code with the procedure code. They must be "reasonable."

V.   Review and update all charge tickets, computer files, and encounter forms annually.

Introduction to Current Procedural Terminology (CPT)

The American Medical Association (AMA) released the first edition of Current Procedural Terminology (CPT) in 1966. It was similar to a coding system developed ten years earlier by the California Medical Association (CMA) called the California Relative Value System (CRVS). These codes were based on a four-digit system. In 1970, the AMA released the Second Edition of CPT, adding a fifth digit to make services more specific. The Third Edition was printed in 1973, and the Fourth Edition in 1977. Also, during this time, many insurance companies developed their own coding systems. Some payers used these coding systems internally and others required the doctor use these special codes to report services to that insurer.

By 1983, a government study identified over 120 different procedure-coding systems. It was impossible to match services in all these different coding systems, so the government mandated a standard coding system for Medicare and Medicaid. Beginning in 1984, HCFA required physicians to report all services in HCPCS for all Medicare and Medicaid claims. Also in 1984, the AMA modified the name of CPT and began including the year in the title.

CPT-1992 changed all the "visit" services, such as office calls, hospital care, and nursing home visits, to "evaluation and management" services. In spite of many articles in medical publications, seminars, and newsletters, some physicians still have trouble determining the exact level of care to use for a patient. While deciding the correct level of service is the responsibility of the physician, not the medical assistant, we will explore these codes in the worksheets. Medicare required this change as part of their implementation of the Resource Based Relative Value Scale (RBRVS) mandated by Congress to reform the Medicare payment structure.

The present edition of CPT contains over 7500 different descriptions of services. The AMA protects these codes and descriptions by a copyright. Look at the introductory pages of the current edition. They give credit to the CPT Panel and Advisory Committees responsible for developing these codes. The Table of Contents shows the organization of the reference. Note that the largest section, as you would expect, is the Surgery listing. Appendix B summarizes the code changes since the last edition. This list identifies the codes you must update in your computer or on office documents. Some CPT vendors and the AMA have editions with color-coded pages, color keys, and thumb indexed pages to make it easier to use. Their terminology and illustration sections can provide guidance with unfamiliar terms. The CPT Index is not complete, but it can help you search for new codes.

Most successful projects start at the beginning. Look at the CPT Introduction. Most of the higher numbered codes, the E/M (evaluation and management) services, appear first since most physicians do these services. Any doctor can report a code from any section, if that is the service performed. However, reasonableness must be tested. Would a podiatrist perform neurosurgery? Not likely, but it could appear that way if you transpose digits in the procedure code. Later, we will work with a worksheet that looks at reasonable code matching. The terminology format, with the stem of the procedure before the semicolon, saves space and makes the page easier to read. This code layout is standard in the CPT, HCPCS and ICD-9-CM references.

Coding Guidelines appear in each CPT section. You must read these carefully to select the correct codes in this workbook. Procedure descriptions may be misleading if you have not read the rules. We will review the "starred" procedures and "separate procedures" in the surgery section. The "modifiers" do just that, they modify a service. They are so important that all modifiers are listed in CPT Appendix A. Complete your reading of the Introduction and review any terminology and anatomy pages. Now you are ready to start the worksheets.

Evaluation and Management Services

The first three worksheets cover the basic medical visit services provided by almost every health care professional. These are the Evaluation and Management (E/M) codes. The service descriptions are complete, but confusing. An understanding of terms is critical to accurate interpretation of the services. You must read the CPT definitions of commonly used terms carefully. If you are responsible for billing and have obsolete codes or descriptions on the office encounter forms, change them immediately. You may find an old code or modifier in your computer system. Delete them only after making certain you do not need them for statistical use. Contact the vendor of your computer system or software to find the correct procedure for handling obsolete codes and modifiers.

There are three to five levels of many E/M codes. Encounter forms may have a cell labeled "New Patient" and code 99201 listed with the description "Level 1." The Guidelines also advise you that the descriptions vary for all Level 1 codes. As you review the instructions, look at the codes used for illustration. The presenting problems, time, and face-to-face clarifications are essential components of the service descriptions. Review the instructions on selecting a level of E/M service with the doctors and other professionals so that the documentation in the patient's medical record matches the service level reported.

CPT Appendix C provides some clinical examples for each level of service. These are identified by specialty and may help you select the correct code. Do not read anything into the case study that is not there. If we assumed that the patient was blind, obese, or had another complicating problem, the level of service might change. Base your interpretation on the information provided, and nothing else.

Remember our earlier reference to policy benefits deciding whether a code would result in payment? The same rules affect modifiers. Medicare allows the modifier -21, prolonged E/M service, when applied to only the high level codes. Other payers may not honor or may have special rules for using a specific modifier.

Following the Guidelines, CPT begins with the E/M codes. You will find explanatory information throughout the section. You must read these instructions. Many worksheet items use this additional material. The reformatted visit codes on the next page show the similarities and contrasts for these services. Some criteria are consistent for most codes. New patient services require all three key components, history, examination, and medical decision making. Established patient services need two of the three key components. The wording of the paragraph on counseling and coordination of care is consistent throughout the E/M codes.

This section, the visit codes, may be the most complex in CPT. From here it will become easier. Again, review the Guidelines and other instructions carefully as they explain the components of each code. Code the worksheets of E/M encounters, described in terms used by physicians, not the CPT committee. You may not agree with the level of the code listed on the answer sheet, but your choice should be from the same group of codes. Aren't we glad that choosing the appropriate level of E/M codes is the responsibility of the doctor and not the coders?

In 1995, the AMA and HCFA released the documentation standards for E/M services. These described the components of the medical history and the number of body areas and organ systems that the doctor must examine and document for each level of service. In 1997, HCFA clarified this list by identifying the mandatory elements of the exam. The doctor supports a detailed exam (99203) by documenting twelve to seventeen exam items. The complexity of medical decision making is also explained. Updated documentation requirements are expected in 2004 or 2005. Be certain there is a copy of these criteria in your office so anyone creating medical records can follow these guidelines. All payers should accept this documentation standard, and the AMA may include it in future editions of CPT.

When the first three E/M services are placed next to each other, it is easier to see the similarities and differences between the codes:

New Patient - 99201

Office or other outpatient visit for the evaluation and management of a new patient, which requires these three key components:

- a problem-focused history;

- a problem-focused examination; and

- straightforward medical decision making.

Counseling and/or coordination of care with other providers or agencies are provided consistent with the nature of the problem(s) and the patient's and/or family's needs.

Usually, the presenting problem(s) are self limited or minor. Physicians typically spend 10 minutes face-to-face with the patient and/or family.

New Patient - 99202

Office or other outpatient visit for the evaluation and management of a new patient, which requires these three key components:

- an expanded problem-focused history;

- an expanded problem-focused examination; and

- straightforward medical decision making.

Counseling and/or coordination of care with other providers or agencies are provided consistent with the nature of the problem(s) and the patient's and/or family's needs.

Usually, the presenting problem(s) are of low to moderate severity. Physicians typically spend 20 minutes face-to-face with the patient and/or family.

New Patient - 99203

Office or other outpatient visit for the evaluation and management of a new patient, which requires these three key components:

- a detailed history;

- a detailed examination; and

- medical decision making of low complexity.

Counseling and/or coordination of care with other providers or agencies are provided consistent with the nature of the problem(s) and the patient's and/or family's needs.

Usually, the presenting problem(s) are of moderate severity. Physicians typically spend 30 minutes face-to-face with the patient and/or family.

Evaluation and Management - I

150pts
good Job!! :)

2003 CPT Codes 99201 - 99239

These codes cover office visits, hospital daily visits, and medical services for patients in hospital observation units. Most physicians use visit codes, and sometimes they make up over 90% of the services performed by that doctor.

Remember, some E/M services may require modifiers.

1. Discussion of medications with patient's family, just before patient left the observation unit — 99218

2. Hospital visit, will discharge patient tomorrow — 99231

3. First visit, multiple complaints, meds for diabetes, arthritis and hypertension reviewed and changed as patient has rash secondary to present combination, also fulgurated wart on left ring finger — 99205

4. Visit with nurse for diabetes education — 99211

5. Six-month follow-up visit for patient # 3 above — 99215

6. First day in observation unit, patient collapsed at shopping mall and continues to have an irregular heartbeat — 99219

7. Admission to hospital for Boy Scout with severe poison ivy — 99221

8. Initial office visit for child with chicken pox — 99212

9. Eight year old girl seen again for severe sore throat and fatigue — 99213

10. Admission to ICU for 72 y/o male with massive cerebral hemorrhage, respiratory failure and coma — 99223

11. Hospital visit for patient with severe reaction (rash, vomiting) to x-ray study dye, medication prescribed — 99223

12. Comprehensive follow-up counseling visit, emotionally upset over child's behavior and marital problems, 3:15 to 4:00 p.m. — 99212

13. 48-year-old male admitted to hospital for chest pain and discharged the same day when all diagnostic studies were within normal limits — 99217

Evaluation and Management - II

2003 CPT Codes 99241 - 99275

Consultations occur when one physician or provider requests the OPINION of another physician or provider. The consultant may perform tests to establish the opinion or may initiate treatment. This term is sometimes misused, as when the "patient consults with the doctor." If the second physician assumes part or all the care of the patient, it is a referral and not a consultation. A surgeon is usually not a consultant, but is expected to take care of the patient's problem. Consultation codes have four subcategories: office/outpatient, inpatient, follow-up inpatient and confirmatory.

1. Office consult for high school senior with a knee injury occurring during the homecoming game   _____

2. Initial hospital consult for male diabetic, back surgery 3 days ago, now has a severe urinary tract infection, emergency procedure scheduled for this afternoon   _____

3. Follow-up inpatient consult for patient not responding to medications and conservative treatment   _____

4. Second opinion for a 35-year-old retarded patient scheduled for a tonsillectomy next week   _____

5. Office consultation for patient questioning planned surgery, procedure not indicated at present   _____

6. Brief inpatient consult to rule out abscessed tooth in post-delivery female   _____

7. ICU consult for elderly female with cardiac arrest during gallbladder surgery, now in a coma   _____

8. Subsequent consult for patient in # 7, now on ventilator with no-code order   _____

9. Office consult for teenager with severe acne   _____

10. Office consult for senior with Alzheimer's and previous stroke, now combative and incontinent   _____

11. Seen again in observation unit, comprehensive history/exam, will transfer to surgeon if not improved in 24 hours   _____

12. Follow-up inpatient consultation, responding well to treatment medication   _____

13. 2nd opinion, considering plastic surgery for extensive facial scarring from auto accident   _____

Evaluation and Management - III

2003 CPT Codes 99281 - 99499

These codes are for Emergency, Pediatric Special Care and Patient Transport, Critical Care, Neonatal and Pediatric Critical Care Services, Nursing Facility, Home, and Miscellaneous visits. They cover special or preventive services that may be exclusions under some insurance policies. Be certain the codes you report accurately reflect the services performed so the insurer can appropriately pay or reject the claim. Some services may be payable only for certain diagnoses or in specified locations.

1. Follow up house call for child recovering from flu _____

2. 1 hr. in ER with 3 year old attacked by pit bull, found unconscious with bruises and scrapes, no suturing required _____

3. Admission of premature infant to NICU _____

4. Annual nursing facility visit _____

5. Initial visit to a home for the mentally retarded to see a patient with recent onset of swelling in hands and feet _____

6. 1 hour conference at day-care center with family and geriatric assessment staff, pending transfer of patient _____

7. Visit to NICU infant, will transfer to nursery tomorrow _____

8. 45 minute telephone conversation with a patient threatening suicide _____

9. Extended follow up visit NICU, unstable 2 month old infant _____

10. Constant attendance, 1.5 hours critical care in ICU, 15 year old male comatose after diving accident _____

11. New patient, annual exam, pilot, age 47 _____

12. Initial exam of infant born at home _____

13. Counseling on risk factors, sexually active fourteen-year-old female, 45 minutes _____

14. Preschool exam for 5 year old seen since infancy _____

15. Initial home visit to discuss care options with family of 88 year old disabled stroke patient, 1 hour _____

Anesthesia Services

2003 CPT Codes 00100 - 01999

Physicians who are not anesthesiologists may report anesthesia services. A doctor may be responsible for the anesthesia when a partner performs a surgical procedure. Some large practices have their own surgery room, performing the same procedures in the office that they would do in the hospital outpatient surgicenter. In some cases, an anesthesiologist may not be available. Medical billers should become familiar with these codes and the rules for using them. These services may be a significant part of your coding work in the future.

Anesthesia uses some special modifiers to indicate the patient's condition, P1 through P6, and some of the usual CPT modifiers. There are also some 99xxx codes that you bill along with the regular anesthesia service when there are special qualifying circumstances. Keep these special rules in mind as you complete the worksheet.

The descriptions do not specify anesthesia, but all answers should come from this section. Watch for case studies that need a modifier or multiple codes.

1. Cervical diskography injection _____

2. Abdominal repair, hernia of the diaphragm _____

3. Delivery of twins, no C-section _____

4. Radiation therapy requiring general anesthesia _____

5. Total joint replacement, left ankle, for severe arthritis _____

6. Open reduction, fracture right humerus _____

7. Burr holes, critical newborn infant _____

8. Dual chamber transvenous pacemaker insertion _____

9. Rhinoplasty, correction of deviated septum _____

10. Mid-thigh amputation, right leg _____

11. Harrington rod implant, spinal cord biopsy _____

12. Rectal endoscopy with biopsy _____

13. Insert umbrella filter, inferior vena cava _____

14. Pectus excavatum repair, four year old male _____

15. Arthroscopy, right shoulder _____

General Surgery Rules

Surgical procedures on the integumentary system begin the extensive surgery section. CPT provides important guidelines for all surgery. Review them carefully. Then consider the information below as you review the worksheet items.

1. Necessary medical care for diagnostic surgery is reported separately. Non-diagnostic surgical services include concurrent medical care by the operating surgeon. Other physicians may report medical care that is unrelated to the surgical service. Example: A patient undergoing gallbladder surgery is followed by an internist for chronic emphysema. The internist is paid for the medical care as it is not related to the surgical service. Medicare has comprehensive tables identifying, by procedure code, the days of medical care included in a surgical service. Other insurers may have similar restrictions.

2. Surgical services usually include the local anesthesia administered by the operating surgeon.

3. The payment for the surgery includes all related supplies. The doctor may bill for supplies only if they exceed what is usually required for that service. Insurers may refuse to pay for any additional supplies provided by the surgeon. If the surgery is done in the hospital setting, either inpatient or outpatient, insurers assume the hospital provided all the necessary supplies.

4. The subsection information contains the special instructions for using a particular range of codes. In some cases, this vital information may appear on the previous page. Always, after you find the code you seek, review the previous page or two for any special rules related to this coding section.

5. A service that is usually part of another service may, on occasion, be reported as the primary surgery. These codes appear throughout CPT and the description ends with "(separate procedure)." If you perform a service with the (separate procedure) notation, report that service if it is the ONLY service performed or is unrelated to the other procedures or services performed. This is a rule many doctors find confusing.

6. Starred procedures are often overlooked in billing. Generally, starred services are surgery only codes. They do not include the preoperative or postoperative care. The rules are complicated so read this section carefully. While they are usually minor services, the patient or the doctor is entitled to payment for them.

7. Surgical destruction is usually included in the primary procedure.

8. Use the unlisted procedure code at the end of each surgery section when there is no code for the service performed. New procedures are reported with these codes until a specific code is assigned. If the service involves a new technique for an established procedure, you would usually report the service with the existing code. Note that all unlisted procedure codes end in '9' and many end in '99.' Remember, whenever you report these unlisted services, you will need to attach operative notes or provide a complete description of the service.

9. The special report is similar to the unlisted procedure. Again, you must explain the service completely. Documentation must be sent with the claim. These claims may not be sent electronically as they require attachments.

10. Some of the CPT surgery modifiers are listed in the "Guidelines" of the surgery section. All CPT modifiers appear in Appendix A.

11. Some complications may be reported separately from the surgery using the modifier –22 and a detailed explanation. Medicare will usually reject any medical care billed by the surgeon

during the specified post-operative period. To get paid, the surgeon must establish that the medical care rendered is not part of the usual postoperative care for the previous surgery.

12. Modifiers -54, -55, and -56 cover situations where the surgeon does not provide all the medical care related to the surgery. Physicians, other than the surgeon, may provide and be paid for medical care related to the surgery if the surgeon indicates his service does not include the preoperative or postoperative medical care.

13. Sometimes the doctor performs multiple procedures. If the surgery is a bilateral carpal tunnel release, you may be instructed by the payer to report the code and the modifier –50, or report two identical lines, one with modifier –RT and the other with modifier -LT. Suppose the patient has gall bladder surgery and the doctor also removes nevi from the neck and left thigh, and a basal cell CA of the scalp. You would report the major procedure on the first line, the basal cell CA on the second line, and the nevi on subsequent lines in the order of diminishing significance. The modifier -51 would be used on all but the first service line. Exception: see 15 below. Also, each service line must show the appropriate diagnosis code or reference number.

14. Therapeutic surgery includes all related medical care. The modifier -24 is used when there is a separate, postoperative medical service, unrelated to the surgical procedure. Example: a patient had a surgery last week but now visits the surgeon's office for an acute asthma attack. If the asthma is unrelated to the surgery, the office visit may be billed as a separate service with modifier -24.

15. Some multiple surgical procedures must be reported without modifier -51. These are the "add on" codes, identified in CPT Appendix D. Because these codes are added on to the reporting of another code, they can never be used alone. When printing paper claim forms, be sure that these codes do not roll over to be the only service on another claim form.

16. CPT Appendix E lists the CPT codes that are not "add-on" codes but do not require the modifier –51. Codes such as 20900 (Bone graft, any donor site, minor or small) or 62284 (Injection procedure for myelography) are billable but assumed to be related to another reported service. In fact, Medicare rejects these codes as incorrectly reported if a –51 modifier is attached.

Modifiers increase in importance each year. Each new edition of CPT and HCPCS bring changes in the familiar ones and new modifiers. Be certain you review the modifier sections when you look for changes in procedure codes.

Medicare rejects "unbundling," the coding of multiple services when one code includes all procedures. When physicians code from a list, they may miss a code that contains multiple services. Encounter forms or coding sheets may state:

51840 Marshall-Marchetti

58150 Abdominal Hysterectomy

58700 Salpingectomy(ies)

58940 Oophorectomy(ies)

Turn to code 58150. The description includes codes 58700 and 58940. Suppose the patient with the abdominal hysterectomy also had a Marshall-Marchetti type procedure. The correct code, 58152, contains all the procedures listed above. HCFA (CMS) has revised the rebundling lists several times. Many insurance carriers implement these policies as soon as CMS releases them.

Caution: The CPT worksheets may require multiple procedure codes, a modifier, or the reporting of quantity. Anytime the CPT code says "each," you need to report a quantity, even if it is only one. As you complete the worksheets, pronounce the terms. You can increase your vocabulary as you expand your coding skills.

Integumentary System

These codes include procedures on the skin, subcutaneous and accessory structures, nail, and breast. They cover the removal of lesions, suturing, plastic repairs, burn treatment, and other surgeries. Read the embedded instructions immediately under the headings "Removal of Skin Tags" and "Shaving of Epidermal or Dermal Lesions." Would we report suturing with the shaving of a dermal lesion? No, because the notation states that "the wound does not require suture closure."

Look at CPT's Rule 2 for repairing multiple lacerations. We add together the length of all wounds in the same classification and report the total as a single item. But this rule does not apply to excising multiple lesions as each is reported individually. A ruler with both inches and centimeters will help you report the correct codes for lesions and suturing.

Before beginning the worksheets, look at the codes and read the text of the entire integumentary section. You may wish to have a medical dictionary and anatomy reference handy. Benign lesions are listed before malignant; suturing is simple, intermediate, and complex; and the miscellaneous categories list services that do not fit into other sections. The integumentary system ends with procedures on the breast.

Note: Watch for worksheet items requiring a modifier, quantity, or multiple codes.

Integumentary System

2003 CPT Codes 10021-19499

1. Hair transplant, 21 punch grafts   _____

2. Removal of 8 skin tags from left forearm   _____

3. Implant Norplant contraceptive capsules   _____

4. Simple blepharoplasty, right upper lid   _____

5. Reclosure, three surgical wounds   _____

6. Debridement of skin and subcutaneous tissue, left forearm   _____

7. Permanent removal distal half, left great toenail   _____

8. Full thickness graft 2x5 cm., left cheek   _____

9. Simple right shoulder biopsy, single skin lesion   _____

10. Adjacent tissue transfer, trunk, 8 sq. cm.   _____

11. Laser destruction, benign 2 cm. facial lesion   _____

12. Excision/Z-plasty repair, 11 sq. cm. forehead lesion   _____

13. Aspiration, breast cyst, right   _____

14. Surgical treatment of burn with escharotomy, 4%, 11 y/o female   _____

15. Wound suture, 3/4" right hand, 1/2" left foot   _____

16. Breast reduction, left   _____

17. Excision, simple repair, right axillary hidradenitis   _____

18. Xenograft, left thigh, 4 x 8 cm.   _____

19. Excise malignant 1/2" lesion, neck   _____

20. I & D hematoma, left hand   _____

21. Major debridement of burn, both legs, with anesthesia   _____

22. 2nd stage Mohs' procedure, 4 specimens   _____

23. Fx care, debride left thigh, remove gravel, bone spicules   _____

24. Split graft, 2% body area, back, 2 year old male   _____

25. Lipectomy, right buttock   _____

Musculoskeletal System

Three worksheets on the musculoskeletal system cover the largest unit in the surgery section. They describe procedures on the supporting structures of the body such as bone, muscle, and tendon. The first worksheet includes trauma, excision/removal, replantation, grafting, the head, neck and thorax, spine, abdomen, and shoulder. The second worksheet has procedures on the arm, hand and fingers, pelvis and hip joint. The third involves services on the femur, knee, leg, ankle and foot and concludes with casting, strapping, and arthroscopy.

The many rules and definitions appearing within the chapter give specific instructions on coding. Note that the service includes the first cast or traction device. This information is repeated at the start of the casting section. There are also modifiers to identify the service as right or left, and ones that identify specific digits.

Some doctors use the terms "closed" and "open" to describe the fracture rather than the treatment. If you believe this is happening in your office, talk to the doctor and get this clarified before billing the service.

The musculoskeletal system is arranged by body site, from the top down, from the center out. After the general procedures, it is organized:

1.	Head	8.	Forearm and wrist
2.	Neck and thorax	9.	Hand and fingers
3.	Back and flank	10.	Pelvis and hip joint
4.	Spine	11.	Femur and knee joint
5.	Abdomen	12.	Leg and ankle joint
6.	Shoulder	13.	Foot
7.	Humerus and elbow		

Each body site section follows this organization:

1.	Incision	6.	Manipulation
2.	Excision	7.	Arthrodesis
3.	Introduction or removal	8.	Amputation
4.	Repair, revision, reconstruction	9.	Miscellaneous
5.	Fracture and/or dislocation		

Note how many worksheet items in the musculoskeletal section contain the diagnosis. Watch for items that need multiple procedure codes, right, left, finger and toe modifiers, or quantity specified.

Musculoskeletal System - I

2003 CPT Codes 20000-23929

1. Percutaneous needle biopsy, right deltoid muscle _____

2. Partial acromionectomy, left _____

3. Wick monitoring, muscle compartment syndrome, right leg _____

4. Four segment kyphectomy _____

5. Injection service for left TMJ arthrogram _____

6. LeFort II reconstruction, 2 autografts _____

7. Removal of right shoulder prosthesis for replacement _____

8. Fracture of mandible, dental fixation, closed _____

9. Maxillectomy, intra-extra oral osteotomy, for cyst _____

10. Radical sternal resection with major bone graft for osteomyelitis (two codes) _____

11. Remove external wire fixation under anesthesia _____

12. Open fractures, two thoracic vertebrae _____

13. Right shoulder arthrodesis, no graft _____

14. Care of simple nasal fracture _____

15. Right total shoulder _____

16. Reattachment of total amputation of right thumb tip _____

17. Posterior osteotomy, diskectomy, 2 thoracic vertebrae (two codes) _____

18. Medrol injection, right hip _____

19. Exploratory arthrotomy, left A-C joint _____

20. Open treatment blowout fracture, right orbit _____

21. Microvascular anastomosis, osteocutaneous flap, left great toe _____

22. Custom prosthesis preparation, left ear _____

23. Explore right chest, multiple gunshot wounds _____

24. Incision deep soft tissue, osteomyelitic abscess, left buttock _____

25. Exploration of fusion, lumbar spine _____

Musculoskeletal System - II

2003 CPT Codes 23930-27299

1. Open repair of left Dupuytren's contracture   _____

2. Hypothenar opponensplasty, right   _____

3. Open Bennett fracture with external fixation, left   _____

4. Secondary flexor repair/graft, right no man's land   _____

5. Synovial biopsy of right elbow by arthrotomy   _____

6. Manipulation lunate dislocation, closed   _____

7. Darrach procedure, left   _____

8. Decompression fasciotomy, extensor, left wrist   _____

9. Fx left olecranon, external fixation, open treatment   _____

10. Right Z-plasty fasciectomy with release of 3rd and
    4th IP joints (multiple codes)   _____

11. Repair nonunion of left radius without graft   _____

12. Treatment of traumatic left hip dislocation, no anesthesia   _____

13. Flap repair, syndactyly, right 4th web space   _____

14. Removal of recurrent ganglion, left wrist   _____

15. Transmetacarpal reamputation, left first finger   _____

16. Subfascial soft tissue biopsy, right forearm   _____

17. Manipulation with pin, left epicondylar fracture   _____

18. Closed manipulation MP dislocation left 4th finger, with anesthesia   _____

19. Saucerization distal phalanx, left ring finger   _____

20. Total hip replacement, right   _____

21. Remove implant, revise arthroplasty, left wrist   _____

22. Opposition fusion and graft, left thumb   _____

23. Microvascular toe-to-hand transfer 2nd and 3rd toe to previous bone
    graft, left hand   _____

24. Right femur, epiphyseal arrest by stapling   _____

25. Reinsert ruptured left distal triceps tendon with graft   _____

Musculoskeletal System - III

2003 CPT Codes 27301-29999

1. Right shoulder arthroscopy with lysis of adhesions _____
2. Phalangectomy, left third toe _____
3. Exploration with synovial biopsy by arthrotomy, left knee _____
4. Release of left tarsal tunnel _____
5. Left knee arthroscopy, sewing needle removed _____
6. Fracture right medial malleolus, closed, no manipulation _____
7. Surgical correction with fixation, left patellar fracture _____
8. Gastrocnemius neurectomy, left _____
9. Heyman midtarsal capsulotomy, right _____
10. Lengthening bilateral hamstring tendons _____
11. I & D hematoma, left ankle _____
12. Repair of Risser jacket _____
13. Fracture femoral shaft, open with screws, left _____
14. Right Joplin bunion repair _____
15. Repair of severed collateral ligament, right ankle _____
16. Knock-knee osteotomy, left, before closure _____
17. Lengthening, left Achilles tendon _____
18. Plantar fasciotomy, left, by arthroscopy _____
19. Goldwaite procedure for dislocating patella, right _____
20. Manipulation right trimalleolar fracture _____
21. Guillotine amputation, left tibia/fibula _____
22. Application of right long arm splint _____
23. Left sesamoid fracture, closed treatment _____
24. Revision right long leg cast, walker heel applied _____
25. Right great toe IP joint arthrodesis _____

Respiratory System

From nosebleed and tonsillectomy to removal of a lung, this section covers procedures associated with the nose, sinuses, larynx, trachea, bronchi, lungs, and pleura.

In this system we are introduced to endoscopy. Note that when a surgical or therapeutic endoscopy is performed, the appropriate sinusotomy, diagnostic endoscopy, and inspecting all sinuses is included. This is another example of correct coding, or bundling of services.

This endoscopy section had significant changes in both the 1994 and 1995 editions of CPT. Codes revised in 1994 were deleted in 1995 and replaced with new codes. Things have been fairly stable since then.

Respiratory System

2003 CPT Codes 30000-32999

1. Partial removal, left turbinate _____

2. Split cricoid laryngoplasty _____

3. Endoscopy with A&P ethmoidectomy _____

4. Closure nasoseptal perforations from cocaine _____

5. Bronchoscopy with laser destruction of lesions _____

6. Tube thoracostomy for empyema _____

7. External arytenoidopexy _____

8. Revision of tracheostoma _____

9. Parietal pleurectomy _____

10. Intranasal antrotomy _____

11. Plastic repair closure of tracheostomy _____

12. Intrathoracic tracheoplasty _____

13. Tracheostomy tracheobronchoscopy _____

14. Direct laryngoscopy with biopsy, via microscope _____

15. Surgical nasal endoscopy, polypectomy _____

16. Secondary major rhinoplasty _____

17. Removal of toy from nose, 2 y/o male, in office _____

18. Pneumonolysis with packing _____

19. Radical neck, partial laryngectomy for CA _____

20. Sinusotomy, four sinuses _____

21. Polypectomy, office surgery _____

22. Empyemectomy _____

23. Surgical endoscopy, repair sphenoid CSF leak _____

24. Thoracoscopy, bilateral wedge resection _____

25. Puncture aspiration, left lung _____

Cardiovascular System

This section lists the surgical procedures on the vascular and cardiac systems; the heart, veins, and arteries. The instructional introductory paragraphs refer to first, second, and third order vessels and vascular families, and the injection procedures for arteriography.

The Society of Cardiovascular & Interventional Radiology (SCVIR) distributes an excellent reference explaining the family trees of the vascular system. This manual is available from:

> SCVIR
> 10201 Lee Highway, Suite 160
> Fairfax, VA 22030
> Attn: Coding Users' Guide

Because surgery on the cardiovascular system usually represents major surgery, there are few starred procedures or codes identified as "separate procedure." Operations on the arteries and veins include the arteriogram. Aortic procedures include the sympathectomy, if performed. Diagnostic cardiac catheterization is in the Medicine section.

Review the extensive explanation of pacemaker and cardioverter-defibrillator services. Coronary bypass grafting, both venous and arterial, is complex and requires careful reading.

Caution: Watch out for worksheet item 3. Move slowly and carefully through this CPT section.

Cardiovascular System

2003 CPT Codes 33010-37799

1. Long and short saphenous vein stripping, left leg   _____
2. Vein graft repair, left brachial artery   _____
3. Coronary bypass grafts, 1 venous and 2 arterial   _____
4. Direct repair of vertebral artery aneurysm   _____
5. Revision of pacemaker pocket   _____
6. Removal of fragment, broken arterial catheter   _____
7. Open atrial septostomy with bypass   _____
8. Insertion AV sequential pacemaker   _____
9. Needle placement, left jugular vein   _____
10. Removal of implanted arterial infusion pump   _____
11. Pulmonary embolectomy without bypass   _____
12. Mitral valvotomy with bypass   _____
13. Cardiectomy with heart transplant   _____
14. Intracatheter AV shunt for dialysis   _____
15. Diagnostic arterial puncture   _____
16. Cutdown venipuncture, infant   _____
17. Splenorenal bypass, synthetic graft   _____
18. Percutaneous transluminal fem-pop atherectomy   _____
19. Direct repair of ruptured splenic artery aneurysm   _____
20. Intrauterine fetal transfusion   _____
21. Repeat pericardiocentesis   _____
22. Repair lacerated aorta with bypass   _____
23. Resection with commissurotomy for infundibular stenosis   _____
24. Ligation/Repair patent ductus arteriosus, 19 y/o female   _____
25. Patch closure of ventricular septal defect   _____

Hemic and Lymphatic - Mediastinum and Diaphragm

These combined, small sections include procedures on the spleen, bone marrow, lymph nodes and channels, mediastinum, and diaphragm.

Compared to the cardiovascular section, this one is easy.

CPT 2003 added bone marrow and stem cell services/procedures to this section. Watch for these notations as you code this worksheet.

Hemic and Lymphatic - Mediastinum and Diaphragm

2003 CPT Codes 38100-39599

1. Superficial needle biopsy of inguinal lymph node _____

2. Complete right axillary lymphadenectomy _____

3. Repair acute traumatic hernia of diaphragm _____

4. Insertion of thoracic duct cannula _____

5. Drainage of single lymph node abscess, left axilla _____

6. Thoracoabdominal repair, hiatal hernia _____

7. Excision of deep axillary node, right _____

8. Radical retroperitoneal lymphadenectomy _____

9. Lymphangiotomy _____

10. Mediastinoscopy with biopsy _____

11. Partial splenectomy for traumatic injury _____

12. Superficial inguino-femoral lymphadenectomy _____

13. Retroperitoneal staging lymphadenectomy _____

14. Correct newborn diaphragmatic hernia, insert chest tube _____

15. Needle bone marrow biopsy _____

16. Suprahyoid lymphadenectomy _____

17. Eventration of paralytic diaphragm _____

18. Deep jugular node dissection x 3 _____

19. Allogenic bone marrow transplant _____

20. Injection for lymphangiography _____

21. Removal of benign neoplasm from mediastinum _____

22. Staging, partial pelvic lymphadenectomy _____

23. Excise left axillary hygroma, deep neurovascular dissection _____

24. Repair ruptured spleen _____

25. Total pelvic lymphadenectomy by laparoscope _____

Digestive System

This system covers procedures on the mouth, salivary glands, pharynx, adenoids, tonsils, esophagus, stomach, intestines, appendix, rectum and anus, liver, biliary tract, pancreas, abdomen, peritoneum, omentum, and hernia repair.

This diverse section contains endoscopic procedures and refers to the related radiographic supervision and interpretation service. Remember that surgical endoscopy includes diagnostic endoscopy.

Watch for multiple codes and the item that requires a modifier.

Digestive System

2003 CPT Codes 40490-49999

1. I & D peritonsillar abscess _____
2. Flexible esophagoscopy with removal of FB _____
3. Roux-en-Y bypass for obesity _____
4. Fredet-Ramstedt pyloromyotomy _____
5. Transanal hemicolectomy _____
6. Commando glossectomy _____
7. Initial inguinal hernia repair, 4 year old male _____
8. Transsacral proctectomy _____
9. Simple ligature hemorrhoidectomy _____
10. ERCP with pancreatic duct stent _____
11. Stomal colonoscopy for hemorrhage _____
12. Upper GI endoscopy, dilate obstructed outlet _____
13. Staging laparotomy for Hodgkins, with intraoperative tube jejunostomy _____
14. Second stage, primary bilateral cleft lip repair _____
15. Total arch vestibuloplasty _____
16. Subsequent peritoneal lavage _____
17. Rectal stricture dilation under general anesthesia _____
18. Cholecystectomy with cholangiography _____
19. Thoracic closure of esophagostomy _____
20. Flexible sigmoidoscopy for biopsy _____
21. Partial left lobe hepatectomy _____
22. Salivary gland biopsy by incision _____
23. Hepaticoenterostomy, by U-tube _____
24. Removal of dental implant, left mandible _____
25. Plastic repair of pharynx _____

Urinary System

This section includes the procedures on the kidney, ureter, bladder, and urethra. Also transplant services, including the harvesting of the kidney. Urinary endoscopy and other procedures identify special bundling instructions.

Caution: Read the worksheet items carefully. Urethra and ureter can look similar in some forms of the words. Note the different codes for male and female.

One worksheet item has two possible codes. What else do you need to know to find the exact code?

Urinary System

2003 CPT Codes 50010-53899

1. Subsequent urethral stricture dilation, male, age 27   _____

2. Transurethral resection of prostate   _____

3. Closure of traumatic kidney wound   _____

4. Infant meatotomy   _____

5. Cystourethroscopy, fulguration of 1.9 cm. tumor   _____

6. Complete cystectomy, bilateral lymphadenectomy   _____

7. Bowel anastomosis with ureterocolon conduit   _____

8. Repair of ureterovisceral fistula   _____

9. EMG anal sphincter   _____

10. Subsequent dilation urethra, female, age 21   _____

11. Cystourethroscopy, steroid treatment of stricture   _____

12. Suprapubic catheter aspiration of bladder   _____

13. Exploratory nephrotomy   _____

14. Partial excision of left kidney   _____

15. Excision of Cowper's gland   _____

16. Sling procedure for incontinence, male, age 43   _____

17. Ureterolithotomy, stone in upper third   _____

18. Plastic repair of ureter for stricture   _____

19. Litholapaxy, 2.7 cm. calculus   _____

20. Marshall-Marchetti-Kranz procedure   _____

21. Cystometrogram   _____

22. Injection procedure for chain urethrocystography   _____

23. Percutaneous placement of ureteral stent   _____

24. Bilateral pyeloplasty for horseshoe kidney, left   _____

25. Laser contact vaporization of prostate   _____

Male Genital System

These codes identify procedures on the penis, testis, epididymis, tunica vaginalis, scrotum, vas deferens, spermatic cord, seminal vesicles, and prostate.

Watch for the worksheet item that has two possible answers.

Male Genital System

2003 CPT Codes 54000-55899

1. Newborn clamp circumcision   _____
2. Traumatic partial amputation of penis   _____
3. Punch biopsy of prostate   _____
4. Bilateral hydrocelectomy   _____
5. Radical retropubic prostatectomy   _____
6. Urethroplasty, third stage Cecil repair   _____
7. Electroejaculation   _____
8. Implantation of prosthetic testicle   _____
9. Bilateral vasectomy   _____
10. Chemical destruction of penile condyloma   _____
11. Exploration of scrotum   _____
12. Complex scrotoplasty   _____
13. Insertion of radioactive pellet in prostate   _____
14. One stage repair, perineal hypospadias with tube   _____
15. Radical orchiectomy, abdominal exploration   _____
16. Insertion of inflatable penile prosthesis   _____
17. Abdominal vesiculectomy   _____
18. Varicocelectomy with hernia repair   _____
19. Abdominal exploration for undescended testis   _____
20. Plethysmography of penis   _____
21. Biopsy and exploration of epididymis   _____
22. Testicular biopsy via needle   _____
23. Bilateral venous shunt for priapism   _____
24. Complex prostatotomy for abscess   _____
25. Vasovasorrhaphy   _____

Intersex, Female Genital, and Maternity

This section defines intersex surgery; procedures on the vulva, perineum and introitus, vagina, cervix and corpus uteri, oviduct, ovary, and in vitro fertilization. Also included are the services related to delivery, antepartum, and postpartum care.

With CPT 2000, the laparoscopy codes were given new numbers and moved to the specific body system for that service. There are several options for endoscopy in this section. You may need to read the procedure notes to code the vulvar surgery as simple, radical, partial, or complete.

Note the services included in the prenatal or antepartum care. The instructions state: "other visits or services within this time period should be coded separately." This means that if you see a maternity patient for the flu or a burn, and you code it as unrelated to the pregnancy, you may bill it as an additional service. Would you bill inpatient medical care for the time your patient is hospitalized for delivery? No, not for the usual care associated with delivery, but you could report additional care for other complications. Also, another physician, following the patient for an unrelated difficulty, such as a cardiac problem, would bill for regular medical care unrelated to the delivery.

Examine the instructions on partial prenatal care. Note that "abortion," not miscarriage, is the correct term for an incompleted pregnancy. Abortions may be spontaneous, missed, septic, or induced.

Some worksheet items may require multiple codes or quantity indicators.

Intersex, Female Genital, and Maternity

2003 CPT Codes 55970-59899

1. Removal of 3 small leiomyomata by laparoscopy _____

2. Repair of rectovaginal fistula with colostomy _____

3. Intrauterine embryo transfer _____

4. Sex change surgery, female to male _____

5. Cervical LEEP biopsy, small electrode _____

6. Tubal occlusion with ring _____

7. Treatment of second trimester missed abortion _____

8. Cystocele/urethrocele repair _____

9. Chorionic villus sampling by needle _____

10. Laparoscopic excision of pelvic lesions _____

11. Injection of dye for hysterosalpingogram _____

12. Salpingectomy for ectopic pregnancy, by laparoscopy _____

13. Vaginal delivery with tocolysis _____

14. Vaginal excision, 3 uterine fibroids _____

15. Cervical stump excision, repair of pelvic floor _____

16. Vaginal hysterectomy, partial colpectomy, enterocele repair _____

17. Vaginal trachelorrhaphy _____

18. Laser destruction of extensive vaginal lesions _____

19. Complete pelvic exenteration _____

20. Bilateral excision of ovarian cysts _____

21. C-section delivery with postpartum care _____

22. Tubal ligation, 1 day after delivery _____

23. Fascial sling for stress incontinence _____

24. Biopsy perineum, two lesions _____

25. Hysteroscopy, lysis of adhesions _____

Endocrine and Nervous Systems

Procedures on the thyroid, parathyroid, thymus and adrenal glands, carotid body, skull, meninges and brain, spine and spinal cord, extracranial and peripheral nerves, and autonomic nervous system; destruction by neurolytic agent, neuroplasty, and neurorrhaphy are included on this worksheet.

The Nervous System surgery is categorized by approach, definitive surgery, and reconstruction services, and may be performed by more than one surgeon. You may want to refer to an anatomy text for clarification of the complex neurosurgical procedures.

Caution: Worksheet items 6 and 23. Don't forget modifiers and quantity where needed.

Endocrine and Nervous Systems

2003 CPT Codes 60000-64999

1. Subtotal thyroidectomy with radical neck dissection   _____
2. Transcranial orbital exploration, removal of bullet   _____
3. Intra-abdominal avulsion, vagus nerve   _____
4. Laminectomy and excision of intradural sacral lesion   _____
5. Single nerve graft, left arm, 4.5 cm.   _____
6. Injection procedure, lumbar diskogram (L4-L5)   _____
7. Decompressive resection, single cervical vertebral body   _____
8. Remove and replace CSF shunt system   _____
9. Percutaneous stereotactic chemical lesion, trigeminal   _____
10. Excision of thyroid adenoma   _____
11. Paracervical nerve block for delivery   _____
12. Repeat subdural tap through suture   _____
13. Excise and graft of infected intradural bone   _____
14. Total removal of implanted spinal neurostimulator   _____
15. Bone flap craniotomy for cerebellopontine tumor   _____
16. Suture thenar motor nerve, right hand   _____
17. Exploratory burr hole, supratentorial   _____
18. Repair complex dural intracranial AV malformation   _____
19. Cervical hemilaminectomy/re-exploration & decompression   _____
20. Brain stem biopsy, transoral/split mandible approach   _____
21. Excision of carotid body tumor and artery   _____
22. Craniectomy for posterior fossa tumor   _____
23. Cable nerve grafts, 3cm left arm, 4.5 cm left leg   _____
24. LeFort osteotomy with fixation, anterior fossa   _____
25. Cranioplasty for 6.5cm skull lesion   _____

Eye and Ocular Adnexa

This section lists procedures on the eyeball, cornea, iris, ciliary body, lens, vitreous, retina, eye muscles, bony orbit, eyelids, conjunctiva, and lacrimal system.

Note the distinction between ocular and orbital implants. There are many laser procedures for the eye. Removal of a cataract may include other services. The surgeon may do the lens implant as a single stage procedure, at the time the cataract is removed, or later.

To code accurately, what more do you need to know about item 9? Watch for add-on or multiple codes and modifiers.

Eye and Ocular Adnexa

2003 CPT Codes 65091-68899

1. Probe/Irrigate left nasolacrimal duct under general   _____

2. One laser treatment session, 3 small retinal breaks, left   _____

3. Exploration left orbit, remove embedded nailhead   _____

4. Excise .75 cm. conjunctival lesion, left eye   _____

5. Reinsert ocular implant with conjunctival graft, right   _____

6. Revise operative site, right anterior segment   _____

7. Removal of posterior FB with magnet, left eye   _____

8. Left tarsal wedge blepharoplasty for ectropion   _____

9. Iridectomy for glaucoma, left   _____

10. Correction of right surgical astigmatism by wedge   _____

11. External levator repair, right blepharoptosis   _____

12. Enucleation, insertion of muscle stabilized implant, left   _____

13. Repeat scleral buckling, old retinal detachment, left   _____

14. Excise lower lid chalazions, 3 left, 1 right   _____

15. Right corneal laceration repair with tissue glue   _____

16. Laser treatment of left vitreous strands   _____

17. Removal of right dacryolith   _____

18. Laser trabeculoplasty, right   _____

19. Discission of left secondary cataract by incision   _____

20. Total reconstruction, right upper lid   _____

21. Extracapsular phacoemulsification with lens implant, left   _____

22. Posterior fixation for strabismus, resect 2 horizontal muscles, right eye   _____

23. Plug closure, right lacrimal punctum   _____

24. Bilateral antibiotic injection, anterior chamber   _____

25. Initial superior oblique strabismus surgery, left   _____

Auditory System

This section includes procedures on the external, middle and inner ear, and the temporal bone. After the eye, coding the ear services seems easy.

Caution: One worksheet item needs an add-on code, most need modifiers.

Auditory System

2003 CPT Codes 69000-69990

1. Replace left temporal bone conduction device _____

2. Bilateral otoplasty for severely protruding ears _____

3. Total facial nerve repair and graft, by operating microscope _____

4. Repeat right mastoidectomy, now radical _____

5. Excision of right external ear cyst _____

6. Neurectomy, right tympanic membrane _____

7. Postauricular middle ear exploration, left _____

8. Subtotal mastoidectomy, right _____

9. Semicircular canal fenestration, left _____

10. Stapedotomy, repair of right ossicular chain _____

11. Catheterize/Inflate eustachian tube, transnasal _____

12. Right oval window fistula repair _____

13. Facial nerve repair, medial/geniculate, left _____

14. Left tube tympanostomy with Novocain _____

15. Subtotal amputation, right external ear _____

16. Cochlear implant, right _____

17. Excision polyp, left ear _____

18. Remove FB left external ear, general anesthesia _____

19. I&D of abscess, left external meatus _____

20. Myringoplasty, right _____

21. Left mastoidectomy with labyrinthectomy _____

22. Excision of neoplasm, left temporal bone _____

23. Mastoidectomy/tympanoplasty, reconstruct Rt ossicular chain _____

24. Excision left extratemporal glomus tumor _____

25. Routine cleaning of right mastoid cavity _____

Radiology

The first worksheet of radiographic procedures covers the section on diagnostic radiology and imaging. It includes flat films of the head and neck, chest, spine, pelvis, upper and lower extremities. These studies are the most common radiologic procedures performed in the physician's office.

Worksheet II includes studies of the abdomen, gastrointestinal and urinary tracts, and gynecological and obstetrical services. It also includes diagnostic imaging of the heart, aorta and arteries, and veins and lymphatics. It concludes with transcatheter procedures, transluminal atherectomy, and other procedures.

The third worksheet covers three sections. The first section, diagnostic ultrasound or "echo" includes procedures for diagnosis and guidance. The second section, radiation oncology, provides codes for clinical treatment planning, delivery and management, hyperthermia, and brachytherapy. The last section, diagnostic nuclear medicine, has codes for the endocrine, lymphatic, gastrointestinal, musculoskeletal, cardiovascular, respiratory, nervous, and genitourinary systems, and therapeutic nuclear studies.

Radiology services, the 70000 codes, are one of the non-surgical sections in CPT. The section has special instructions, unlisted procedure codes, and modifiers. The "supervision and interpretation" services correspond to many of the injection procedures in previous surgical sections. Many of the "S&I" codes are followed by a reference to the surgical part of the diagnostic service. The Interventional Radiology Coding Users' Guide is very helpful in explaining these services.

Many specialists perform S&I studies, not just radiologists. Note that a written report, signed by the doctor interpreting the study, is part of the service and may not be billed separately. Nuclear medicine, once limited to the hospital setting, is now part of some medical practices.

Remember that the service at the doctor's office is the global or complete service. The same study performed at the hospital must be reported as the "professional component." With very few exceptions, when the place of service is 21 (inpatient), 22 (outpatient), or 23 (emergency department), the 7xxxx service will require the modifier –26.

Move slowly through this section, reading all instructions and definitions. If you are confused by words ending in "gram" or "graphy," think of telegram and telegraphy. One is the result, the other the process.

Watch for items requiring modifiers or multiple codes.

Radiology - I

2003 CPT Codes 70010-73725

1. S&I arthrography, left knee   _____
2. 4 views, nasal fracture   _____
3. X-ray of right knee, 4 views   _____
4. CT of pelvis, with contrast   _____
5. Neck CT with contrast and additional sections   _____
6. Pelvis, 2 views   _____
7. X-ray left eye, no foreign body   _____
8. Scoliosis x-ray study of the spine   _____
9. Chest x-ray, 1 view   _____
10. TMJ arthrography, with supervision/interpretation   _____
11. S&I pacemaker insertion   _____
12. 2 views right 4th and 5th fingers   _____
13. Cervical MRI, no contrast   _____
14. X-ray teeth, right upper, left upper and lower   _____
15. 2 views cervical spine, outpatient   _____
16. Right left x-ray, 2 month old baby boy   _____
17. Bilateral fractured ribs, 3 views   _____
18. X-ray elbow, PA and Lateral   _____
19. Complete study left hip   _____
20. Head MRI, no contrast, inpatient   _____
21. X-ray exam left scapula, 3 views   _____
22. CT thoracic spine with contrast   _____
23. Proton imaging for lymph nodes, chest   _____
24. X-ray right sialolith   _____
25. Cervical myelogram, S&I   _____

Radiology - II

2003 CPT Codes 70400-76499

1. CT guidance for stereotactic localization _____
2. Bilateral selective adrenal venography, S&I _____
3. Videography of swallowing _____
4. Acute abdomen series _____
5. Cineradiography in operating room _____
6. Bilateral selective adrenal angiography, S&I _____
7. Supervise/Interpret voiding urethrocystography _____
8. Bilateral femoral intravascular ultrasound _____
9. S&I, Transcatheter removal of broken catheter _____
10. LeVeen shuntogram S&I _____
11. Barium enema, KUB study _____
12. Contrast monitoring to change percutaneous drain tube, S&I _____
13. S&I bilateral carotid neck angiogram _____
14. Retrograde urography with KUB _____
15. Percutaneous transhepatic portography, S&I, in ER _____
16. S&I, transluminal renal atherectomy _____
17. Supervise/Interpret AV shunt angiogram _____
18. S&I Bilateral selective renal angiography _____
19. Thoracic aortography by serialography, S&I _____
20. Perineogram _____
21. Lymphangiography, right arm, S&I _____
22. Consult/Report on x-rays done at University Hospital _____
23. Orthoroentgenogram _____
24. Bilateral mammogram _____
25. Percutaneous gastrostomy tube placement, S&I _____

Radiology - III

2003 CPT Codes 76506-79999

1. Complete obstetrical B-scan, twin pregnancy _____
2. Thyroid, metastatic CA imaging, total _____
3. Simulation treatment planning, right hip and knee _____
4. SPECT cardiac rest and exercise studies at hospital _____
5. Lymph gland imaging _____
6. Residual urinary bladder study _____
7. Radiation treatment: L shoulder & hip, 7.5 MeV _____
8. Pulmonary ventilation and perfusion study, quantitative _____
9. Transrectal echo _____
10. Intracavitary element placement, 11 ribbons, outpatient _____
11. Combined B-12 absorption study _____
12. Radioelement placement, surface of left forearm _____
13. Ophthalmic biometry A-scan _____
14. External hyperthermia, 2.7 cm. deep _____
15. Splenic red cell survival measurement _____
16. First pass cardiac resting study _____
17. Brachytherapy planning, two sources _____
18. SPECT bone imaging, professional component only _____
19. Provision of diagnostic isotope _____
20. Ultrasound guidance for needle biopsy, S&I _____
21. Radionuclide localization, lung abscess _____
22. PET tumor imaging, professional component _____
23. Repeat fetal Doppler echocardiogram _____
24. Ultrasound guidance for amniocentesis, S&I _____
25. SPECT liver imaging _____

Pathology and Laboratory

Lab worksheet Part I covers lab panels, drug testing, therapeutic drug assays, evocative/suppression testing, clinical pathology consultations, urinalysis, and ends with chemistry tests. Note that the chemistry tests are listed in alphabetic order.

Part II includes molecular diagnostics, hematology, coagulation, immunology and tissue typing.

The final lab worksheet describes transfusion medicine, microbiology, anatomic pathology, including postmortem examination and cytopathology, cytogenics, surgical pathology, and miscellaneous laboratory services.

Reimbursement varies widely for laboratory studies. Review the manuals for the office testing equipment to determine the correct code for each study. Do not take the word of the equipment salesperson.

A federal regulation, the Clinical Laboratory Improvement Act (CLIA), rated laboratory tests by complexity. Each lab is certified to perform a specified level of testing. Some physician's offices discontinued laboratory work altogether. Other practices reduced their laboratory work to only basic, uncomplicated services.

As you complete the worksheets, review the Guidelines and look for instructions within each subsection. A few codes include the physician's services. Watch for the lab tests with legal implications. Unlike the surgical services, the clinical laboratory tests may be numbered so that the lowest code number identifies the most comprehensive study. A few even describe testing you can do safely at home.

Some worksheet items require multiple codes or quantity reporting.

Pathology and Laboratory - I

2003 CPT Codes 80048-83887

1. Four studies each, lutenizing hormone and FSH   _____
2. Quantitative theophylline screen, blood   _____
3. Occult blood in stool, two simultaneous guaiac tests   _____
4. Qualitative cystine/homocystine, urine   _____
5. Urinary amino acids, quantitative, 3 specimens   _____
6. Glucose tolerance test, 4 specimens   _____
7. Blood ethanol levels   _____
8. Semen analysis for fructose   _____
9. Atomic spectroscopy, manganese   _____
10. HDL cholesterol direct measurement   _____
11. Manual microscopic urinalysis   _____
12. Blood catecholamines   _____
13. Creatinine clearance   _____
14. Obstetric panel of tests   _____
15. Hemoglobin, methemoglobin, qualitative   _____
16. Folic acid RBC   _____
17. Cocaine drug screening   _____
18. Estriol   _____
19. Color pregnancy test, urine   _____
20. Total serum cholesterol   _____
21. Hepatitis ABC antibodies, B surface antigens   _____
22. Fractionation (17-KS) ketosteroids   _____
23. CRH stimulation panel   _____
24. Mucopolysaccharide screen   _____
25. TSH panel, 4 studies, two hours   _____

Pathology and Laboratory - II

2003 CPT Codes 83890-86849

1.   Total blood protein, Western Blot   _____
2.   Quantitative D-dimer degraded fibrin   _____
3.   PKU blood test, 2 day old infant   _____
4.   Routine prothrombin time   _____
5.   Vitamin E   _____
6.   Total T cell with absolute CD4 and 8   _____
7.   Single nucleic acid probe   _____
8.   Eastern equine encephalitis antibody test   _____
9.   Clotting factor VIII, single stage   _____
10. Vitamin B-2   _____
11. C-reactive protein   _____
12. Parathyroid hormone   _____
13. Heparin neutralization   _____
14. HLA typing, A, single antigen   _____
15. Strip test, urea nitrogen   _____
16. Skin test for histoplasmosis   _____
17. Chorionic gonadotropin, qualitative   _____
18. Hepatitis C antibody   _____
19. Total testosterone   _____
20. Platelet antibody identification   _____
21. Urinary potassium   _____
22. Total clotting inhibitor, protein S   _____
23. Blood/urine Xylose absorption test   _____
24. Rubella antibody screen   _____
25. Double strand DNA antibody   _____

Pathology and Laboratory - III

2003 CPT Codes 86850-89399

1. Platelet pooling
2. Bone marrow tissue analysis for malignancy
3. Scanning electron microscopy
4. Stool culture for Salmonella
5. Coroner ordered autopsy
6. Surgical pathology, gross/micro, uterus with tumor
7. Flow cytometry, DNA analysis
8. Rabbit inoculation, observation
9. Influenza detection by immunoassay
10. Gross autopsy, including brain
11. Surgical pathology, gross/micro cholesteatoma
12. Preoperative autologous blood collection/storage
13. Complete semen analysis
14. Consult/report on slides from University Hospital
15. Antibiotic sensitivity study, 10 disks
16. Chlamydia culture
17. Limited chromosome analysis/banding, amniotic fluid
18. KOH skin slide prep
19. Forensic cytopathology for sperm
20. CSF cell count with differential
21. Thawing fresh frozen plasma, 2 units
22. Three hour gastric secretory study
23. Preparations for nerve teasing
24. Collection of vaginal smear for dark field exam
25. Intraoperative consultation and frozen section, two specimens

Medicine

Worksheet I covers injections, psychiatry, dialysis services, diagnostic medical services for gastroenterology, and non-surgical procedures on the eye and ear. Many psychotherapy codes were updated in 1998.

The second worksheet has cardiovascular and pulmonary diagnostic and therapeutic services, procedures for allergy, and neurology.

Worksheet III includes chemotherapy and physical medicine. The special services of Osteopaths and Chiropractors, additional anesthesia codes, and other services are the final subsections of CPT. The recently added Category III codes may not be accepted by all insurance plans. Some of the special services, procedures and report also may be excluded from payment.

Many CPTs ago, office visits were part of the Medicine section. Then they became evaluation and management services and are now listed separately. The invasive procedures in this section are diagnostic and are usually considered non-surgical. This may seem strange since coronary angioplasty, the procedure some people have instead of open-heart surgery, is in this section. Others have noticed this anomaly. In November 1993, Medicare announced that angioplasty, and several other services would be treated as surgery and all routine medical care would be included in the procedure.

Many doctors use services from this section such as injections, EKGs, and pulmonary function testing. Generally, as you can see from the subsection listing, these services belong to a medical specialty. Study these services carefully. The Guidelines for this section are familiar. Now we apply them to medical procedures rather than surgery.

Caution: Watch for multiple codes, modifier, and quantity reporting.

Medicine - I

2003 CPT Codes 90281-92700

1. Endothelial microscopy, cell count, photo/report _____
2. Medical hypnotherapy to stop smoking _____
3. Intravenous injection _____
4. Glaucoma water provocation test with tonogram _____
5. Rhinomanometry _____
6. Binaural hearing aid exam _____
7. Manometric studies, anus and rectum _____
8. Bernstein test for esophagitis _____
9. Tangent screen visual fields, right eye _____
10. Tetanus vaccine, 27 year old male, jet injector _____
11. Hepatitis B immunization series, 18 y/o dialysis patient _____
12. Biofeedback training for arrhythmia _____
13. Monthly dialysis monitoring, 16 y/o female _____
14. Psychotherapy, 1 hour, 15 minutes _____
15. Psychotherapy with family, patient absent _____
16. Comprehensive eye exam, new patient _____
17. Fluorescein angiography, complete _____
18. Contact lens replacement, right _____
19. Tympanometry _____
20. Dialysis training, one session _____
21. Air audiometry _____
22. Fitting of bifocal lenses _____
23. Multiple seizure electroconvulsive treatments, two days _____
24. Audiometry by select picture _____
25. Inpatient nonverbal psychotherapy with medical visit, 45 minutes _____

Medicine - II

2003 CPT Codes 92950-96004

1. Coronary thrombolysis by IV infusion   _____
2. Inpatient right and left heart cath, congenital heart defect   _____
3. Interp/Report only, tilt table cardiac testing   _____
4. Pulmonary percutaneous balloon valvuloplasty   _____
5. EMG/NCT, cranial nerve supplied muscles, bilateral   _____
6. Dispense 15 doses antigen, bee & wasp   _____
7. Brief study, transcranial Doppler   _____
8. Cardiac stress test, tracing only   _____
9. Awake/sleep EEG, 10 p.m. to 7 a.m.   _____
10. CPAP   _____
11. Scratch tests, 10 trees, 3 venom   _____
12. Skin electromyography, 10 muscles, running on treadmill   _____
13. 24 hour ECG, miniature, recording only   _____
14. Complete service, 1 month patient activated spirometry recording   _____
15. Repeat analysis of cranial nerve stimulator implant   _____
16. Myasthenia gravis tensilon test   _____
17. His Bundle recording   _____
18. Interpret/Report total body plethysmography   _____
19. Venous Doppler, both legs, complete study   _____
20. Transesophageal echocardiogram, total service   _____
21. Ear oximetry for O2 saturation   _____
22. S&I for cardiac cath with angiography   _____
23. Stress echocardiogram, complete   _____
24. Complete ambulatory blood pressure monitoring   _____
25. Electrical testing of blink reflex   _____

Medicine - III

2003 CPT Codes 96100-0044T

1. Nurse visit to patient's home for urinary catheter change _____
2. Poisoning treatment with Ipecac, observation _____
3. Iontophoresis, 35 minutes _____
4. Limited developmental testing with report _____
5. OMT, head and neck _____
6. IV conscious sedation _____
7. Endovascular repair of aortic dissection _____
8. Acupuncture, 4 needles _____
9. New patient visit, starred procedure performed _____
10. DEXA analysis, bilateral hips _____
11. Telogen/antigen counts on hair clipped at the lab _____
12. Dexterity testing, hand, 30 minutes, with report _____
13. Behavior intervention, 30 minutes, twins and both parents _____
14. Three hours medical testimony _____
15. Initial visit for newborn born at home _____
16. Scalpel wound debridement, two sessions _____
17. Reevaluation of physical therapy treatment _____
18. Diabetic meal planning education, 1 hour, 4 patients _____
19. Home visit and enema for fecal impaction _____
20. Medical meniscus transplant, right knee, by arthroscopy _____
21. Chemotherapy, arterial infusion, 55 minutes _____
22. Gait and stairs retraining, 30 minutes _____
23. IM chemotherapy administration _____
24. Chiropractic treatment, 2 spinal areas _____
25. Two home visit infusions, 5 y/o with hemophilia _____

HCPCS Level II Codes

Developed by the Health Care Financing Administration (now CMS), HCPCS (Healthcare Common Procedure Coding System) National Level II codes identify over 2400 codes and descriptive terminology for services not included in CPT. HCPCS (pronounced "hick-picks") provides codes for reporting supplies, injections, and the services of non-physician providers such as ambulance companies and dentists. HCPCS code changes start on January 1 with CPT.

Level II HCPCS codes begin with a letter followed by four digits. Originally designed for Medicare and Medicaid, private insurers are beginning to accept and understand these codes. There were also Level III HCPCS codes. These began with W, X, Y, or Z, and were established by each Medicare carrier. Because of this, Level III codes were excluded from the HCPCS Level II code reference. The standardization of codes sets required by the Health Insurance Portability and Accountability Act of 1996 (HIPAA), eliminated the use of Level III codes.

HCPCS lists codes alphabetically. Some Level II sections are unusual. There are no K codes in the index because K codes are used only for DMERCS (Durable Medical Equipment Regional Carriers). Many M (medical) services eventually appear in CPT. Q codes are temporary codes, sometimes appearing midyear when it becomes necessary to identify a service previously included in or reported by another code. Medicare and Medicaid bulletins will tell you when to report a new Q code.

Read the Introduction for an explanation of the HCPCS reference. Each of the sections begins with "Guidelines" on how to use the codes correctly. There may be a mini-index to that section. The index may show a single code, a range of codes, or provide no indication of that service. Like the CPT index, you may need to think of other ways to describe the service if you are to find the correct code.

HCPCS modifiers appear in Appendix A or 1, and a summary of code changes in Appendix B or 2. There are two sorted lists in HCPCS, a table of drugs (Appendix C or 3) and a general index. Appendix D (or 4) is a list of deleted codes. Many private companies print versions of this codebook. Your reference may differ in format but the codes and descriptions should be consistent with all vendors. These companies may provide an expanded index or additional information on the use of these codes.

As you code the worksheet, start with the index. Then verify the code(s) with the actual code section as there may be sizes, quantities, or other variables in selecting the correct code. Read the "Guidelines" to be certain you select the proper code. Many terms are similar and may be unfamiliar. If you use these codes in your work, consult with your employer to be certain you report the correct code.

HCPCS has special two letter modifiers. Some of these are included in the Modifier worksheet.

HCPCS Level II Codes

2003 HCPCS

1. Evaluation for hearing aid _____
2. Two inch thick cushion for wheelchair _____
3. Injection, 1.2 million units Bicillin C-R _____
4. Premolded removable metatarsal support, right foot _____
5. Chelation therapy _____
6. Kit for collagen skin test _____
7. Ladies surgical boot, right foot, orthopedic aftercare _____
8. Single root canal, right upper incisor _____
9. Injection, 8 mg. Compazine _____
10. Preschool screening for language problems _____
11. Vinyl urinary bag with tube and leg strap _____
12. Custom made plastic artificial eye _____
13. Obtained Pap smear, sent to lab _____
14. Methotrexate, 50 mg. _____
15. Non-emergency transportation by wheel-chair van _____
16. Nasogastric tubing, no stylet _____
17. Adjustable aluminum three prong cane, with tips _____
18. Sterile gloves, one pair _____
19. Mitomycin 60 mg. _____
20. Took x-ray to nursing home, 1 patient seen _____
21. Dorrance hook hand prosthesis, model 6 _____
22. Injection, Estradiol, 9 mg. _____
23. Needleless injection device _____
24. Toronto orthosis for Legg Perthes _____
25. Apnea monitor, high risk infant _____

Modifiers

Modifiers are two character suffixes for procedure codes. They provide important information on how that service changed in some way without altering the definition of the code. Using modifiers properly eliminates some of the need to send procedure notes with claims. All CPT modifiers are two digit numbers and HCPCS modifiers are two letters or a letter and digit. Some modifiers apply to evaluation and management services only while others clarify surgical procedures. Both CPT and HCPCS list some relevant modifiers before some code sections and provide a complete list of modifiers in Appendix A.

CPT modifiers may indicate a reduced or expanded service, bilateral procedures, or the professional component of a service. HCPCS modifiers may indicate the rental or purchase of a piece of equipment, services by a social worker, or that the services were provided in a medically underserved area. Medicare and Medicaid may also direct you to apply HCPCS modifiers to CPT codes. Like the codes they modify, modifiers may be changed or eliminated with each new edition of CPT or HCPCS.

Appendix A shows the modifiers as -22 or -AN. The "-" is not usually reported but is useful if you write out a code as "12345-22" or "54321-LT." The claim form has a special column for modifiers. Some payers may ask you to report modifiers as a five-digit code, 09922 or 099LT. The worksheet requires a modifier for each scenario. Use Appendix A in the CPT and HCPCS codebooks to select the correct two-character modifier. Some items may require multiple answers.

Modifiers

Name _____

2003 CPT

1. The patient had major surgery by Dr. Jones on July 16, and saw the doctor on August 4 for an unrelated office visit. The August 4 service requires modifier: _____

2. Dr. Brown asks Dr. White to assist him at a major surgery because a surgery resident is not available. Dr. White reports the surgery code with modifier: _____

3. When an insurer requires a presurgical second opinion, the service is reported with the modifier: _____

4. The surgery was difficult because the patient was a paraplegic weighing 427 pounds. To report these circumstances to the insurer, use modifier: _____

5. Dr. Gray, the family doctor, asks a surgeon, Dr. Green to see Mrs. Brown at City Hospital as she may need surgery. Dr. Green schedules the surgery for tomorrow and reports today's service with modifier: _____

6. Dr. Thomas does an appendectomy and removes a mole from the patient's neck while in the OR. Use modifier ___ on the ___ service line of the claim form. _____

2003 HCPCS

7. Dr. Reed, a clinical psychologist, saw a Medicare patient for diagnostic testing. Dr. Reed reports 96100 with modifier: _____

8. If you refile a claim and change the procedure code because it was incorrect on the original claim, use modifier: _____

9. When a procedure is recorded on an analog tape recorder, use modifier QT. For a digital recording use: _____

10. Dr. Johns takes the x-ray but Dr. Hopkins does the interpretation and report. Identify the modifiers for both doctors: _____

11. Dr. Little sees patients in an inner city clinic, serving in a Health Personnel Shortage Area (HPSA). He receives additional compensation for these services by reporting modifier: _____

12. Mr. Small obtains a cane from the medical supply store. If it was a new cane, report modifier: _____

Introduction to ICD-9-CM

Diagnosis coding systems are older than procedure coding methods. Almost one hundred years ago a French physician developed a system for coding causes of death. At the turn of the century, the U. S. Public Health Service (PHS) began using the same codes. In 1950, the PHS and the Veterans Administration (VA) adopted ICD-8, the International Classification of Disease, Eighth Revision, Adapted. The World Health Organization (WHO) developed ICD-8 in the late 1930s. With the U.S. implementation of ICDA-8 (ICD Adapted), our information on mortality could be matched with statistics from the rest of the world.

Non-governmental hospitals began to use ICDA-8, and the PHS expanded the system to include codes for surgery and treatment. Private agencies were also developing coding structures and by the 1960s the U. S. used at least two diagnosis coding systems. In 1979, the government mandated the use of a new system, ICD-9-CM for reporting services to Medicare and Medicaid.

The ICD-9-CM, International Classification of Disease, Ninth Revision, Clinical Modification, is compatible with the WHO system, ICD-9. Congress required a standardized coding system for the implementation of DRGs, Diagnosis Related Groups, in 1983. The DRGs are Medicare's hospital payment method. All the diagnoses in ICD-9-CM are grouped into less than 500 DRGs. The hospital receives payment for the patient's DRG category, not the cost of the patient's care.

After the government standardized the diagnosis coding system, many private organizations started printing ICD-9-CM with improvements. Some place a color-coded box over the numbers that need a 4th or 5th digit; some distribute the codes in a ring binder; another has anatomical drawings throughout that illustrate the codes. You may buy a loose-leaf subscription for updated pages from some agencies. The government no longer prints an annual edition of ICD-9-CM, and does warn that they are not responsible for the errors made by others in printing the codes.

ICD-9-CM updates codes on a quarterly basis but if the office buys a new book after the October printing date, it should be safe to use for the next year. The publishers usually print the year prominently on the cover so you know when the book becomes obsolete. If the office subscribes to an update service for a loose-leaf ICD-9-CM, remember the October date, as you may not notice if you fail to receive the new pages.

The doctor's office uses two of the three volumes of ICD-9-CM. Volume 1, the Tabular List, provides the codes by body system, in numeric order. Volume 2, the Alphabetic Index, contains many diagnoses that are missing in the Tabular List. After finding the diagnosis in Alphabetic Index, Volume 2, it must be verified with Tabular List, Volume 1. If you use only the Alphabetic Index, you may select an incorrect code. For convenience, these are frequently printed with the alphabetical index first. Volume 3 of ICD-9-CM contains procedure codes used by hospitals. The doctor's office uses CPT for reporting services, not Volume 3.

Many physicians' offices use only 50 to 100 diagnosis codes. Rather than look them up each time, codes appear on encounter forms or "cheat sheets" used by the billers. There are two problems with this approach. First, the list restricts the number of diagnoses available. Do all the patients have only two or three kinds of hypertension? Second, the office must update the codes on an annual basis. Maybe they review these codes only when they need to order encounter forms. Unfortunately, if you order forms in August or September, your forms may not have the updated codes required for the next year.

It seems reasonable to assume that with all the updating of codes, we will eventually need a completely new system. ICD-10-CM is coming but the U. S. will delay its implementation until at least the year 2006 or beyond. The HIPAA mandated changes must be implemented before we can consider ICD-10-CM. Until then, you must become familiar with ICD-9-CM.

Using ICD-9-CM

The office may code either the principle diagnosis or the primary diagnosis for the patient visit. The principle diagnosis is the condition found after study. The primary diagnosis is the reason for the visit. Suppose you see a patient complaining of abdominal pain. If you can establish the cause, such as acute appendicitis, you may report that code. If the complaints are vague, maybe the flu, the threat of layoffs at work, or an upcoming week of final exams, the doctor may code "abdominal pain" for the office visit. Hospitals use the principle diagnosis.

While using CPT, we found very few services described by a person's name, an eponym. A medical term or anatomical description identified most procedures. One exception to this rule is bunion surgery where proper names are used to differentiate surgical techniques, such as Mitchell, Keller, McBride, etc. Diagnoses frequently use a person's name, Parkinson's or Cushing's disease, or a Bennett fracture. This is probably because the diagnosis coding system is older and diseases were traditionally named for the physician first reporting the condition.

Like CPT, you will need to become familiar with the coding conventions of ICD-9-CM. The medical office should observe the rules on "includes" and "excludes" but we have limited use for the "code also underlying disease." Before beginning the worksheets, take time to review the introduction, the terminology, and the format of the Tabular and Alphabetic volumes. Some editions of ICD-9-CM are specifically designed for coding in the doctor's office. If you are fortunate enough to have one of those, read all the preliminary information for many helpful hints on using ICD-9-CM.

Diagnosis Coding - Quick and Dirty

Billers receive many invitations to attend seminars on the fine art of diagnosis coding. The instructors are frequently medical records people who must be exact in their hospital reporting. They emphasize accuracy above all else. Unfortunately, it is not that easy in the doctor's office. The diagnosis coding system was developed to collect information worldwide on the presence of disease. We must use the same system to defend charging for medical services. As an example, there are few problems not made worse by obesity. Since obesity is not the problem we are treating, it is not mentioned. If fact, many insurers would not pay for any service billed with the diagnosis of obesity.

Also, the doctor's office may be limited to only one diagnosis per service. We simply must select the "best" diagnosis code for the service. Diagnosis codes must be reasonable for the service performed. Always subject your coding to a reasonableness test. The next worksheet will show you how. The answers appear after the Ten Commandments of Diagnosis Coding. The HCFA Official Guidelines for Coding and Reporting appear after the Reasonableness Test.

Reasonableness Testing

Procedures and diagnoses must be reasonable; they must match each other. No one will declare it reasonable to x-ray a foot for a broken wrist. To assure that your choices come from the correct sections, the summary tables are presented below.

Diagnoses

1. 001-139   Infectious/Parasitic Disease
2. 140-239   Neoplasms
3. 240-279   Endocrine/Nutrition/Immunity
4. 280-289   Blood/Blood Forming Organs
5. 290-319   Mental Disorders
6. 320-389   Nervous System/Sense Organs
7. 390-459   Circulatory Systems
8. 460-519   Respiratory System
9. 520-579   Digestive System
10. 580-629   Genitourinary System
11. 630-677   Pregnancy/Childbirth
12. 680-709   Skin/Subcutaneous Tissue
13. 710-739   Musculoskeletal/Connective Tissue
14. 740-759   Congenital Anomalies
15. 760-779   Perinatal Conditions
16. 780-799   Symptoms/Signs/Ill-Defined Conditions
17. 800-999   Injury/Poisoning
18. V01-V83   Health Status/Contact V-codes
19. E800-E999   External Causes E-codes

Procedures

1. 99201-99499   Evaluation/Management
2. 10021-19499   Integumentary System
3. 20000-29999   Musculoskeletal System
4. 30000-32999   Respiratory System
5. 33010-37799   Cardiovascular System
6. 38100-39599   Hemic/Lymph/Mediastinum
7. 40490-49999   Digestive System
8. 50010-53899   Urinary System
9. 54000-55899   Male Genital System
10. 55970-59899   Intersex/Female/Maternity
11. 60000-64999   Endocrine/Nervous Systems
12. 65091-68899   Eye/Ocular Adnexa
13. 69000-69990   Auditory System
14. 70010-79999   Radiology Services
15. 80048-89399   Pathology Services
16. 90281-99600   Medical Services
17. 0001T-0044T   Category III Codes

Using these tables, we can determine "reasonable" coding sections for procedures and diagnoses. If we assume there are no significant complications, we can select the reasonable code ranges for a fractured finger:

Diagnoses: Musculoskeletal (13), Injury (17), External Causes (19)
Procedures: E/M (1), Musculoskeletal (3), Radiology (15)

Using the code section numbers, identify diagnoses and procedures for:

1. Headache: Diagnoses:

                  Procedures:

2. Pneumothorax: Diagnoses:

                  Procedures:

3. Ulcer: Diagnoses:

                  Procedures:

ICD-9-CM
Official Guidelines For Coding and Reporting

Effective October 1, 2002. Narrative changes appear in bold text.

A. Selection of first-listed condition. In the outpatient setting, the term first-listed diagnosis is used in lieu of principal diagnosis. In determining the first-listed diagnosis the coding conventions of ICD-9-CM, as well as the general and disease specific guidelines take precedence over the outpatient guidelines. Diagnoses often are not established at the time of the initial encounter/visit. It may take two or more visits before the diagnosis is confirmed. The most critical rule involves beginning the search for the correct code assignment through the Alphabetic Index. Never begin searching initially in the Tabular List as this will lead to coding errors.

B. The appropriate code or codes from 001.0 through V83.89 must be used to identify diagnoses, symptoms, conditions, problems, complaints, or other reason(s) for the encounter/visit.

C. For accurate reporting of ICD-9-CM diagnosis codes, the documentation should describe the patient's condition, using terminology which includes specific diagnoses as well as symptoms, problems, or reasons for the encounter. There are ICD-9-CM codes to describe all of these.

D. The selection of codes 001.0 through 999.9 will frequently be used to describe the reason for the encounter. These codes are from the section of ICD-9-CM for the classification of diseases and injuries (e.g. infectious and parasitic diseases; neoplasms; symptoms, signs, and ill-defined conditions, etc.).

E. Codes that describe symptoms and signs, as opposed to diagnoses, are acceptable for reporting purposes when a diagnosis has not been established (confirmed) by the physician. Chapter 16 of ICD-9-CM, Symptoms, Signs, and Ill-defined conditions (codes 780.0 - 799.9) contain many, but not all codes for symptoms.

F. ICD-9-CM provides codes to deal with encounters for circumstances other than a disease or injury. The Supplementary Classification of factors Influencing Health Status and Contact with Health Services (V01.0- V83.89) is provided to deal with occasions when circumstances other than a disease or injury are recorded as diagnosis or problems.

G. Level of Detail in Coding

1. ICD-9-CM is composed of codes with either 3, 4, or 5 digits. Codes with three digits are included in ICD-9-CM as the heading of a category of codes that may be further subdivided by the use of fourth and/or fifth digits, which provide greater specificity.

2. A three-digit code is to be used only if it is not further subdivided. Where fourth-digit subcategories and/or fifth-digit subclassifications are provided, they must be assigned. A code is invalid if it has not been coded to the full number of digits required for that code. See also discussion under Section I, General Coding Guidelines, Level of Detail.

H. List first the ICD-9-CM code for the diagnosis, condition, problem, or other reason for encounter/visit shown in the medical record to be chiefly responsible for the services provided. List additional codes that describe any coexisting conditions.

I. Do not code diagnoses documented as "probable", "suspected," "questionable," "rule out," or "working diagnosis". Rather, code the condition(s) to the highest degree of certainty for that encounter/visit, such as symptoms, signs, abnormal test results, or other reason for the visit.

Please note: This differs from the coding practices used by hospital medical record departments for coding the diagnosis of acute care, short-term hospital inpatients.

J. Chronic diseases treated on an ongoing basis may be coded and reported as many times as the patient receives treatment and care for the condition(s).

K. Code all documented conditions that coexist at the time of the encounter/visit, and require or affect patient care treatment or management. Do not code conditions that were previously treated and no longer exist. However, history codes (V10-V19) may be used as secondary codes if the historical condition or family history has an impact on current care or influences treatment.

L. For patients receiving diagnostic services only during an encounter/visit, sequence first the diagnosis, condition, problem, or other reason for encounter/visit shown in the medical record to be chiefly responsible for the outpatient services provided during the encounter/visit. Codes for other diagnoses (e.g., chronic conditions) may be sequenced as additional diagnoses.

For outpatient encounters for diagnostic tests that have been interpreted by a physician, and the final report is available at the time of coding, code any confirmed or definitive diagnosis(es) documented in the interpretation. Do not code related signs and symptoms as additional diagnoses.

Please note: This differs from the coding practice in the hospital inpatient setting regarding abnormal findings on test results.

M. For patients receiving therapeutic services only during an encounter/visit, sequence first the diagnosis, condition, problem, or other reason for encounter/visit shown in the medical record to be chiefly responsible for the outpatient services provided during the encounter/visit. Codes for other diagnoses (e.g., chronic conditions) may be sequenced as additional diagnoses.

The only exception to this rule is that when the primary reason for the admission/encounter is chemotherapy, radiation therapy, or rehabilitation, the appropriate V code for the service is listed first, and the diagnosis or problem for which the service is being performed listed second.

N. For patient's receiving preoperative evaluations only, sequence a code from category V72.8, Other specified examinations, to describe the pre-op consultations. Assign a code for the condition to describe the reason for the surgery as an additional diagnosis. Code also any findings related to the pre-op evaluation.

O. For ambulatory surgery, code the diagnosis for which the surgery was performed. If the postoperative diagnosis is known to be different from the preoperative diagnosis at the time the diagnosis is confirmed, select the postoperative diagnosis for coding, since it is the most definitive.

P. For routine outpatient prenatal visits when no complications are present codes V22.0, Supervision of normal first pregnancy, and V22.1, Supervision of other normal pregnancy, should be used as principal diagnoses. These codes should not be used in conjunction with chapter 11 codes.

The Ten Commandments of Diagnosis Coding

An irreverent summary of rules with practical coding hints

I. The largest number of digits wins.

Do not report three if there are four, do not report four if there are five.

II. Numeric codes win over alphanumeric.

If the code is listed twice, once with a letter and once with all numbers, use the one with all numbers, if possible.

III. Watch out for punctuation.

Do not even think it. Do not think "427 point 0" or "250 point 00." These codes are 4270 and 25000. Many claim form scanners and electronic claim programs cannot process the punctuation mark.

IV. Use only the code(s) related to the services performed.

A patient with acute bronchitis and heart disease is seen for the bronchitis. The chart indicates it is time for an ECG. If you code the ECG for bronchitis, it may not pay. With Medicare, it could result in a "not medically necessary" rejection.

V. Diagnosis coding does not raise the payment, only allows it.

A "better" diagnosis will not raise the payment. The neck can be x-rayed for pain, arthritis, or cervical fracture, all will allow payment. The diagnosis of foot pain, even if treated at this office visit, does not justify a neck x-ray.

VI. Do not code in greater specificity than the information provided.

Do not code "rule out" and "suspected" as if the condition existed. The patient is seen because she thinks she broke her hand. If related to an accident and when the x-ray does not confirm a fracture, code "pain" or "contusion" or "traumatic injury."

VII. Neoplasms are always benign, unless stated to be malignant. If malignant, they are always primary, unless stated to be secondary or in situ.

Some lesion codes are general, others are found in the neoplasm table. When using the table, be certain to select the correct column and verify that code with the Tabular List. Do not give the patient something he does not have.

VIII. Always verify codes selected from the Alphabetic Index with the Tabular List.

IX. Diagnosis codes in the Tabular List, in italics, cannot be used as the primary diagnosis.

These codes are listed as "excludes" or "code also the underlying disease." Be certain the correct code is selected and verified.

X. Sometimes the best diagnosis code is going to be the one that is least incorrect.

60

Diagnosis Coding Worksheet Instructions

This workbook divides ICD-9-CM into sections, each with two worksheets. Exercise I requires the use of the Tabular List. Study the code section of the Tabular List and record the appropriate THREE-DIGIT category indicator for where you would find that condition listed. Your search may be easier if you look in the ICD-9-CM Appendix E for the three-digit categories. Then go to the Tabular section for verification of your choice. Always read the introductory Notes at the beginning of each section to find the basic rules for the codes in that category.

The second exercise requires a search of the Alphabetic Index and verification of the code in the Tabular volume. Some diagnosis codes require a 5th digit that may not be easy to find in the Alphabetic Index.

Take the time to look around the reference volumes as you use them. Some of the worksheet codes have very unusual codes listed near them. Would you believe there is a diagnosis called "no room at the inn"? Can you guess what it means? Look it up and see if you were right.

Answers to the Reasonableness Test:

1. Diagnosis: 5, 6, 7, 8, 13, 16
   Procedure: 1, 3, 11, 14, 16

2. Diagnosis: 8, 16, 17
   Procedure: 1, 4, 14, 16

3. Gotcha! There isn't enough information here to code this one. Is it a skin ulcer, mouth ulcer, or abdominal ulcer? Identify all the ulcer types you can think of, and code them all for diagnoses and procedures.

Infectious/Parasitic Diseases - I (001-139)

2003 ICD-9-CM

These diseases are generally considered communicable or transmissible. It also includes a few diseases of unknown or possibly infectious origin. You must use caution with these codes as they can affect employment possibilities, such as identifying a communicable disease for a food handler, a cook, or a waiter. A person's ability to obtain life or health insurance can be affected by a report of one of these diseases, and there could be other significant consequences. This section contains the codes for AIDS, ARC, and HIV used to register patients with the Center for Disease Control (CDC).

Using the Tabular List only, identify the three-digit category for:

1. Salmonella _____

2. Hepatitis _____

3. Late effects of polio _____

4. TB of central nervous system _____

5. Herpes simplex _____

6. Mumps _____

7. Trench mouth _____

8. HIV with Kaposi's Sarcoma _____

9. Gangrene _____

10. Warts _____

Infectious/Parasitic Diseases - II (001-139)

Using the alphabetic and/or tabular references, locate the following diseases and code to acceptable specificity, three, four, or five characters.

1. Acute viral conjunctivitis with hemorrhage   _____

2. Death from bite of wild dog   _____

3. Seven day Queensland fever   _____

4. Lyme Disease   _____

5. Ringworm   _____

6. Trichomonal fluor   _____

7. Congenital syphilitic osteomyelitis   _____

8. E coli intestinal infection   _____

9. Dandy fever   _____

10. Ground itch   _____

11. Hiss-Russell shigellosis   _____

12. Haverhill streptobacillus   _____

13. Pseudocowpox   _____

14. Subacute spongiform encephalopathy   _____

15. Paratyphoid fever   _____

16. Rubella encephalitis   _____

17. Australian X disease   _____

18. Pulmonary paracoccidioidomycosis   _____

19. Intestinal tuberculosis found in sputum   _____

20. Schaumann's lymphogranulomatosis   _____

21. Early macular leprosy   _____

22. Lupus tuberculosis   _____

23. Herpetic felon   _____

24. African eyeworm infection   _____

25. Monkey malaria   _____

Neoplasms - I (140-239)

2003 ICD-9-CM

Coders frequently have trouble with neoplasms. Accuracy is critical if the doctor plans to enroll the patient in one of the cancer registry services. A Johns-Hopkins representative told of finding that over 50% of the patients in their tumor registry did not have the cancer specified in their enrollment records. Referring physician errors on the registration documents caused Johns-Hopkins to send the doctors information on treating the wrong kind of tumor.

Read the instructions for this section very carefully. The Alphabetic Index contains a neoplasm table. This is the starting place when you look for a neoplasm code. The table has a separate code for primary, secondary, and CA in situ. The Tabular List arranges the codes by body site, in a similar sequence as the neoplasm table. As a general practice, avoid coding "uncertain behavior" and "unspecified." Try to hold any claim until you know the type of neoplasm. If you code malignant, and it is benign, it may be very difficult to get the records changed. If you code benign and it is malignant, you may not receive the correct payment.

Caution: There is a "trick" question on the worksheet. Read the instructions carefully!

Using the Tabular List only, identify the three-digit category for:

1. Malignant neoplasm of tongue   _____

2. Benign neoplasm of tongue   _____

3. Skin carcinoma in situ   _____

4. Leukemia   _____

5. Malignant neoplasm of pancreas   _____

6. Kaposi's Sarcoma   _____

7. Breast carcinoma in situ   _____

8. Neoplasm, nature unknown   _____

9. Lung malignancy   _____

10. Bladder cancer   _____

Neoplasms - II (140-239)

Using the alphabetic and/or tabular references, locate the following diseases and code to acceptable specificity, three, four, or five characters.

1. Ventriculi carcinoma   _____

2. Primary cancer of the cauda equina   _____

3. Tumor of the lip   _____

4. Carcinoma in situ, thalamus   _____

5. Tumor of coccyx, secondary to brain cancer   _____

6. Neurofibroma, abdominal wall skin   _____

7. Cancer of the brain   _____

8. Metastasis to Zuckerkandl's organ   _____

9. Unspecified tumor of Cowper's gland   _____

10. Benign tumor of the left eyebrow   _____

11. Metastatic carcinoma of the omentum   _____

12. Uterine malignancy   _____

13. Benign neoplasm renal pelvis   _____

14. Polycythemia vera   _____

15. Mesocolonic malignancy   _____

16. Pancreatic glucagonoma   _____

17. Lymphangioendothelioma   _____

18. Malignant neoplasm of submaxillary gland   _____

19. Tracheal carcinoma in situ   _____

20. Benign tumor of thymus   _____

21. Non-Hodgkin's lymphoma   _____

22. Benign tumor of breast, male   _____

23. Cancer of the respiratory system   _____

24. Retrobulbar malignancy, left eye   _____

25. Glossopalatine fold carcinoma   _____

Endocrine, Nutritional, Metabolic, Immunity Disorders - I (240-279)

2003 ICD-9-CM

This section deals with diseases NOT caused by tumor. These are some of the most common reasons for a visit the doctor's office. Many of these conditions are hereditary, many last a lifetime. Many contribute to health complications as we age. As a wise man once said, "Most people die of the cumulative effects of heredity, lifestyle and environment."

Using the Tabular List only, identify the three-digit category for:

1. Hyperlipidemia   _____

2. Diabetes   _____

3. Thyrotoxicosis   _____

4. Vitamin D deficiency   _____

5. Dwarfism   _____

6. Obesity   _____

7. Beriberi   _____

8. Testicular dysfunction _____

9. Acute thyroid disease   _____

10. Gout   _____

Endocrine, Nutritional, Metabolic, Immunity Disorders - II (240-279)

Using the alphabetic and/or tabular references, locate the following diseases and code to acceptable specificity, three, four, or five characters.

1. Proliferative diabetic retinopathy   _____

2. Addison's disease   _____

3. Xylulosuria   _____

4. Pickwickian syndrome   _____

5. Glucoglycinuria   _____

6. Hashimoto's disease   _____

7. Diabetic coma   _____

8. Lymphatism   _____

9. Graves' disease   _____

10. Pendred's syndrome   _____

11. Diabetic (ketoacidosis) coma, insulin dependent   _____

12. Forbes-Albright syndrome   _____

13. Pseudopseudohypoparathyroidism   _____

14. Iatrogenic hyperinsulinism   _____

15. Nezelof's syndrome   _____

16. Adenomatous thyroid cyst with storm   _____

17. Mild malnutrition   _____

18. Urbach-Wiethe syndrome   _____

19. Sporadic goitrous cretinism   _____

20. Uric acid nephrolithiasis   _____

21. Respiratory alkalosis   _____

22. Alcoholic pellagra   _____

23. Struma nodosa   _____

24. Night blindness due to vitamin deficiency   _____

25. Acute rickets   _____

Blood and Blood-Forming Organs - I (280-289)

2003 ICD-9-CM

This section covers diseases of the blood and blood forming organs. Anemia and clotting disorders are the most common.

Using the Tabular List only, identify the three-digit category for:

1. Christmas disease   _____

2. Cooley's anemia   _____

3. Infantile pseudoleukemia   _____

4. Marchiafava-Micheli syndrome   _____

5. Imerslund's syndrome   _____

6. Aplastic anemia NOS   _____

7. Hereditary hyposegmentation   _____

8. Sideropenic dysphagia   _____

9. Emotional polycythemia   _____

10. Megakaryocytic hypoplasia   _____

Blood and Blood Forming Organs - II (280-289)

Using the alphabetic and/or tabular references, locate the following diseases and code to acceptable specificity, three, four, or five characters.

1. Antithromboplastinemia _____
2. Paroxysmal cold disease _____
3. Massive blood transfusion thrombocytopenia _____
4. Lipophagocytosis _____
5. Impoverished blood _____
6. Siderotic splenomegaly _____
7. Hemoglobin S disease _____
8. Plummer-Vinson disease _____
9. Autoimmune cold sensitivity _____
10. Iron deficiency anemia _____
11. Blood dyscrasia _____
12. Lederer-Brill syndrome _____
13. Vitamin K deficiency _____
14. Lazy leukocyte syndrome _____
15. Classical hemophilia _____
16. Zurich hemoglobin disease _____
17. Splenic hyperemia _____
18. Sclerothymic hyperviscosity syndrome _____
19. Idiopathic allergic eosinophilia _____
20. Thrombocytopathy _____
21. Thalassemic variants _____
22. Blackfan-Diamond syndrome _____
23. Hypoleukia splenica _____
24. Consumption coagulopathy _____
25. Goat's milk anemia _____

Mental Disorders - I (290-319)

2003 ICD-9-CM

Read the introduction carefully. Notice the exclusion of diseases with an organic origin. This section includes psychoses, neuroses, conduct disorders, and retardation.

Caution: Worksheet item 20 on the next page.

Using the Tabular List only, identify the three-digit category for:

1. Neurasthenia   _____
2. Senile dementia   _____
3. Paranoia   _____
4. Voyeurism   _____
5. Anorexia nervosa   _____
6. Schizophrenia   _____
7. Pyromania   _____
8. Dipsomania   _____
9. Dyslexia   _____
10. Delirium tremens   _____

Mental Disorders - II (290-319)

Using the alphabetic and/or tabular references, locate the following diseases and code to acceptable specificity, three, four, or five characters.

1. Hypochondriac _____
2. Organic brain syndrome _____
3. Panic agoraphobia _____
4. Korsakoff's alcoholic psychosis _____
5. Munchausen's syndrome _____
6. Catatonic schizophrenia in remission _____
7. Pseudocyesis _____
8. IQ 27 _____
9. Psychogenic polyarthralgia _____
10. Megalomania _____
11. Hyperactive attention deficit disorder _____
12. Inherited idiocy _____
13. Huntington's dementia _____
14. Manic depressive disorder _____
15. Drug withdrawal syndrome _____
16. Rare emotional insomnia _____
17. Asexual trans-sexualism _____
18. Occasional cocaine abuse _____
19. Acute chronic paranoid schizophrenia _____
20. Frequent leader of 4th grade truancy group _____
21. Shoe fetish _____
22. Dyspraxic syndrome _____
23. Psychogenic dyspareunia _____
24. Subacute infective psychosis _____
25. Active Heller's syndrome _____

Nervous System and Sense Organs - I (320-389)

2003 ICD-9-CM

Inflammatory, hereditary, and degenerative diseases of the central nervous system, as well as disorders of the peripheral nervous system, eyes, and ears are included in this section. Review the table describing the levels of visual impairment and note the difference in the U.S. and WHO definitions of blindness.

Caution: One two-word description may give you different codes depending on which word you look up in the alphabetic index. Both are correct - isn't that interesting?

Using the Tabular List only, identify the three-digit category for:

1. Hemophilus meningitis   _____

2. Pick's disease   _____

3. Jacksonian epilepsy   _____

4. Pseudocyst of the retina   _____

5. Double vision   _____

6. Otitis media   _____

7. Restless legs   _____

8. Meniere's disease   _____

9. Keratoconus   _____

10. Tic douloureux   _____

Nervous System and Sense Organs - II (320-389)

Using the alphabetic and/or tabular reference, locate the following diseases and code to acceptable specificity, three, four, or five characters.

1. Retrolental fibroplasia   _____

2. Pseudomonas aeruginosa meningitis   _____

3. Friedreich's ataxia   _____

4. Spastic ophthalmic artery   _____

5. Late effect of subdural brain abscess   _____

6. Hereditary degenerative keratopathy   _____

7. Mastoid cholesteatoma   _____

8. Familial intention tremor   _____

9. Arcus senilis   _____

10. Multiple sclerosis   _____

11. Guillain-Barre syndrome   _____

12. Vitreous floaters   _____

13. Jamaican neuropathy   _____

14. Amaurosis   _____

15. Morton's neuroma   _____

16. Decreased ocular pressure with papilledema   _____

17. Profound blindness both eyes   _____

18. Romberg's syndrome   _____

19. Brain marasmus   _____

20. Irritation 5th cranial nerve   _____

21. Pseudohole of the macula   _____

22. Tympanosclerosis   _____

23. Pars planitis   _____

24. Crossed eyes, alternating A pattern   _____

25. Soemmering's ring   _____

Circulatory System - I (390-459)

2003 ICD-9-CM

This system includes rheumatic fever and resulting heart disease, hypertensive and ischemic heart disease, diseases of the pulmonary circulation, and other heart diseases. It also includes cerebrovascular disease and diseases of the blood vessels and lymphatics.

Using the Tabular List only, identify the three-digit category for:

1. Aortic insufficiency   _____
2. Ruptured abdominal aortic aneurysm   _____
3. Myocardiopathy   _____
4. Mobitz II block   _____
5. Elephantiasis   _____
6. Postphlebitic syndrome   _____
7. Capillary hemorrhage   _____
8. Buerger's disease   _____
9. Arteriosclerosis   _____
10. Thrombosed hemorrhoids   _____

Circulatory System - II (390-459)

Using the alphabetic and/or tabular references, locate the following diseases and code to acceptable specificity, three, four, or five characters.

1. Sick sinus syndrome _____

2. Anterolateral myocardial infarct _____

3. Kawasaki disease _____

4. Subacute bacterial endocarditis _____

5. Congestive failure with malignant hypertension _____

6. Ruptured berry aneurysm _____

7. Bifascicular block _____

8. Temporal arteritis _____

9. Acute rheumatic endocarditis _____

10. Bilateral stenosis of carotid artery _____

11. Superior vena cava syndrome _____

12. Iliac vein phlebitis _____

13. Rare African cardiomyopathy _____

14. Benign renovascular hypertension _____

15. Atrial flutter _____

16. Paroxysmal atrial tachycardia _____

17. Subclavian steal syndrome _____

18. Transient ischemic attacks _____

19. Infected stasis ulcers _____

20. Cerebrovascular insult _____

21. Nonfilarial chylocele _____

22. Intermittent claudication _____

23. Wolff-Parkinson-White disorder _____

24. Atherosclerosis of coronary artery bypass graft _____

25. Prinzmetal angina _____

Respiratory System - I (460-519)

2003 ICD-9-CM

This system includes acute infections and other respiratory diseases such as pneumonia and influenza, obstructive pulmonary disease, and external causes of lung disease, as well as other forms of lung disorders.

Using the Tabular List only, identify the three-digit category for:

1. Hay fever   _____

2. Hemothorax   _____

3. Detergent asthma   _____

4. Smoker's cough   _____

5. Laryngitis   _____

6. Pleurobronchopneumonia   _____

7. Mediastinitis   _____

8. Pigeon fanciers' disease   _____

9. Sinus polyp   _____

10. Hemophilus pneumonia   _____

Respiratory System - II (460-519)

Using the alphabetic and/or tabular references, locate the following diseases and code to acceptable specificity, three, four, or five characters.

1. Aspiration pneumonia   _____
2. Traumatic nasal septal deflection   _____
3. Idiopathic diffuse interstitial fibrosis   _____
4. Retropharyngeal abscess   _____
5. Broncholithiasis   _____
6. Acute sinus infection   _____
7. Cork handlers' disease   _____
8. Tracheostenosis   _____
9. Postoperative pulmonary edema   _____
10. Croup   _____
11. Allergic rhinitis   _____
12. Radiation fibrosis of the lung   _____
13. E Coli pneumonia   _____
14. Laryngeal muscle spasm   _____
15. Black lung disease   _____
16. Eosinophilic asthma   _____
17. Gangrenous pharyngitis   _____
18. Chronic obstructive pulmonary disease   _____
19. Acute follicular tonsillitis   _____
20. Acute fistular empyema   _____
21. Legionnaire's disease   _____
22. Bullous emphysema   _____
23. Nasopharyngeal inflammation   _____
24. Chlamydia pneumonia   _____
25. Asthmatic bronchitis   _____

Digestive System - I (520-579)

2003 ICD-9-CM

This unit covers diseases of the oral cavity, salivary glands and jaws, esophagus, stomach and duodenum, appendicitis, abdominal hernias, noninfectious enteritis and colitis, and other diseases of the intestines, peritoneum, and digestive system.

Using the Tabular List only, identify the three-digit category for:

1. Alcoholic cirrhosis   _____
2. Impacted wisdom tooth   _____
3. Cholecystitis   _____
4. Duodenal ulcer   _____
5. Sprue   _____
6. Pyloric stenosis   _____
7. Sialolithiasis   _____
8. Crohn's disease   _____
9. Pancreatitis   _____
10. Peritonitis   _____

Digestive System - II (520-579)

Using the alphabetic and/or tabular reference, locate the following diseases and code to acceptable specificity, three, four, or five characters.

1. Hematemesis _____

2. Choledochoduodenal fistula _____

3. Portal thrombophlcbitis _____

4. Pain in right TMJ _____

5. Lingua villosa nigra _____

6. Appendicitis with abscess _____

7. Postgastrectomy diarrhea _____

8. Hemorrhagic pancreatitis _____

9. Acute pyloric ulcer with hemorrhage _____

10. Melena _____

11. Recurrent gangrenous inguinal hernia _____

12. Tooth discoloration from silver _____

13. Toxic parotitis _____

14. Malabsorption syndrome _____

15. Sialodocholithiasis _____

16. Diverticulosis _____

17. Intraoral nasolabial cyst _____

18. Strangulated bowel _____

19. Strawberry disease of the gallbladder _____

20. Functional vomiting _____

21. Retrocecal abscess _____

22. Crohn's intestinal disease _____

23. Gastritis due to alcoholism _____

24. Intussusception of appendix _____

25. Chronic appendicitis _____

Genitourinary System - I (580-629)

2003 ICD-9-CM

This system includes diseases of the kidneys, bladder, ureter, urethra, and male genital organs. Also covered are the diseases of the breast, inflammatory conditions of the female pelvic organs, and female infertility.

Caution: Item 15 on the next page may be a challenge.

Using the Tabular List only, identify the three-digit category for:

1. Renal failure _____

2. Kidney stone _____

3. Acute prostatitis _____

4. Fibrocystic breast _____

5. Polymenorrhea _____

6. Benign prostatic hypertrophy _____

7. Endometriosis _____

8. Female infertility _____

9. Male infertility _____

10. Phimosis (congenital) _____

Genitourinary System - II (580-629)

Using the alphabetic and/or tabular references, locate the following diseases and code to acceptable specificity, three, four, or five characters.

1. Urinary tract infection (UTI) _____
2. Post-hysterectomy vaginal prolapse _____
3. Gynecomastia _____
4. Penile kraurosis _____
5. Infertility from low sperm count _____
6. Salpingo-oophoritis _____
7. Acute pelvic inflammatory disease _____
8. Boil of the scrotum _____
9. Rectovaginal endometriosis _____
10. Breast lump _____
11. Bartholin's gland infection _____
12. Chronic renal failure _____
13. Cervical erosion _____
14. Nephropathy NOS _____
15. Suppurative orchitis _____
16. Membranoproliferative glomerulonephritis _____
17. Floating kidney _____
18. Recurrent urinary fistula _____
19. Chocolate cyst of the ovary _____
20. Pelvic congestive disease _____
21. Balanitis obliterans _____
22. Senile atrophic vaginitis _____
23. Anovulatory infertility _____
24. Subacute nonsuppurative nephritis _____
25. Rupture of corpus luteum cyst _____

Pregnancy, Childbirth, Puerperium - I (630-677)

2003 ICD-9-CM

This unit includes conditions related to ectopic and molar pregnancy, abortive pregnancies, other pregnancy complications; normal delivery, other indications for pregnancy care, and labor and delivery, as well as complications of labor and delivery.

Caution: This is a complicated section. All worksheet II terms must be checked with the Tabular List. Many codes have a required fifth digit. Note the limited options for the fifth digit.

Using the Tabular List only, identify the three-digit category for:

1. Hemorrhoids from pregnancy   _____

2. ABO isoimmunization   _____

3. Ovarian pregnancy   _____

4. Hyperemesis gravidarum   _____

5. Fetopelvic disproportion   _____

6. Cord prolapse   _____

7. Transient hypertension of pregnancy   _____

8. Uterine rupture during labor   _____

9. Twin pregnancy   _____

10. Illegally induced abortion   _____

Pregnancy, Childbirth, Puerperium - II (630-677)

Using the alphabetic and/or tabular references, locate the following diseases and code to acceptable specificity, three, four, or five characters.

1. Severe antepartum thrombophlebitis _____

2. Early separation of the placenta _____

3. Incomplete spontaneous abortion with shock _____

4. Toxemia with convulsions _____

5. Delivery of sextuplets _____

6. Suppressed lactation _____

7. Reopening of C-section wound _____

8. Obstetric shock _____

9. Cardiac arrest from anesthesia for delivery _____

10. Failed attempted abortion with hemorrhage _____

11. Postpartum hemorrhage from retained placenta _____

12. Ruptured fallopian tubal pregnancy _____

13. Prenatal gestational edema _____

14. Gonorrhea, 7th month of pregnancy _____

15. Vaginal hematoma from delivery _____

16. Benign essential hypertension of pregnancy _____

17. Antepartum nephritis _____

18. Cephalopelvic disproportion _____

19. Threatened abortion _____

20. Delivery of fetal death in utero _____

21. Labor complicated by septicemia _____

22. Missed abortion _____

23. Spontaneous breech delivery _____

24. Nursing mother mastitis _____

25. Renal shutdown following elective pregnancy termination _____

Skin and Subcutaneous Tissue - I (680-709)

2003 ICD-9-CM

This section includes infections of the skin and subcutaneous tissue, inflammatory conditions, and other diseases of the skin and subcutaneous tissue.

Using the Tabular List only, identify the three-digit category for:

1. Pressure ulcer   _____

2. Facial boil   _____

3. Ocular pemphigus   _____

4. Paronychia of finger   _____

5. Infected ingrown toenail   _____

6. Poison ivy   _____

7. Baldness   _____

8. Axillary abscess   _____

9. Cafe au lait spots   _____

10. Psoriasis   _____

Skin and Subcutaneous Tissue - II (680-709)

Using the alphabetic and/or tabular references, locate the following diseases and code to acceptable specificity, three, four, or five characters.

1. Dermatitis due to alcohol ingestion _____
2. Nail horn, left thumb _____
3. Lichen-type eruption of axilla _____
4. Hives from allergy to trees _____
5. Wilson-Brocq disease _____
6. Erythema multiforme _____
7. Rhus _____
8. Cheloid scar _____
9. Furunculosis, left temple _____
10. Asteatosis cutis _____
11. Polymorphous eruption from tanning booth _____
12. Infected corn, right foot _____
13. Alligator skin, recent onset _____
14. Senile dermatosis _____
15. Diaper rash _____
16. Granuloma pyogenicum _____
17. Hutchinson's cheiropompholyx _____
18. Solar photosensitivity _____
19. Gibert's disease _____
20. Angioma serpiginosum _____
21. Impetiginous dermatitis _____
22. Abscess both cheeks and chin _____
23. Dermatitis from contact with gold ring _____
24. Chronic neurogenic skin ulcer _____
25. Miliaria rubra tropicalis _____

Musculoskeletal System and Connective Tissue - I (710-739)

2003 ICD-9-CM

This section includes arthropathies and related disorders, dorsopathies, rheumatism (excluding the back), chondropathies, and acquired musculoskeletal deformities. Many codes have a fifth digit. Note that this section excludes fractures.

If you enjoyed coding the musculoskeletal CPT section, you will find this section is even more pleasant. Read very carefully and code only when you are certain of the answer.

Caution: These are large coding lists. You may need information from a previous ICD-9-CM page.

Using the Tabular List only, identify the three-digit category for:

1. Rheumatoid arthritis _____

2. Lumbago _____

3. Knee mice _____

4. Dupuytren's contracture _____

5. Cauliflower ear _____

6. Disseminated lupus erythematosus _____

7. Polymyalgia rheumatica _____

8. Kyphoscoliosis _____

9. Kissing spine _____

10. Hypertrophic pulmonary osteoarthropathy _____

Musculoskeletal System and Connective Tissue - II (710-739)

Using the alphabetic and/or tabular references, locate the following diseases and code to acceptable specificity, three, four, or five characters.

1.	Achilles tenosynovitis	_____
2.	Degenerative polyarticular arthritis	_____
3.	Chondromalacia of the patella	_____
4.	Tennis elbow	_____
5.	Wasting amyotrophy	_____
6.	Degenerative joint disease of the spine	_____
7.	Staphylococcal pyogenic arthritis	_____
8.	Cervical radiculopathy	_____
9.	Old bucket handle tear, lateral meniscus	_____
10.	Swelling in wrist joint	_____
11.	Lordosis following laminectomy	_____
12.	Right plantar fasciitis	_____
13.	Pyomyositis ossificans	_____
14.	Severe bone infection	_____
15.	Calcification of lumbar disc	_____
16.	Pigeon toes	_____
17.	Torticollis	_____
18.	Pectus excavatum, acquired	_____
19.	Post polio foot drop	_____
20.	Flat feet	_____
21.	Bowlegs	_____
22.	Humpback from old age	_____
23.	Low back pain	_____
24.	Kaschin-Beck disease, right ankle	_____
25.	Spontaneous shoulder muscle rupture	_____

Congenital Anomalies - I (740-759)

2003 ICD-9-CM

This section contains conditions that people inherit. These codes differentiate congenital heart disease from acquired heart disease.

Using the Tabular List only, identify the three-digit category for:

1. Anophthalmos   _____
2. Port wine stain   _____
3. Congenital pectus excavatum   _____
4. Bicornuate uterus   _____
5. Missing ear on right   _____
6. Klinefelter's syndrome   _____
7. Ventricular septal defect   _____
8. Cleft lip   _____
9. Congenital hip deformity   _____
10. Pyloric stenosis   _____

Congenital Anomalies - II (740-759)

Using the alphabetic and/or tabular references, locate the following diseases and code to acceptable specificity, three, four, or five characters.

1.   Aphalangia, left foot   _____

2.   Myelomeningocele   _____

3.   Macrodactylism, right thumb   _____

4.   Cauda equina developmental defect   _____

5.   Congenital displacement of the spleen   _____

6.   Cyst of the thyroglossal duct   _____

7.   Alligator skin disease   _____

8.   True dextrocardia   _____

9.   Postductal coarctation of the aorta   _____

10. Achondroplastic dwarf   _____

11. Cryptorchism   _____

12. Endocardial cushion defect   _____

13. Middle ear congenital deformity   _____

14. Premature fontanel ossification   _____

15. Trisomy 21   _____

16. Autosomal dominant polycystic kidney disease   _____

17. Congenital heart block   _____

18. Block-Sulzberger melanoblastosis   _____

19. Fibular hemimelia   _____

20. Ruysch's disease   _____

21. Gillespie's syndrome   _____

22. Supranumery first rib   _____

23. Ambisexuality   _____

24. Amyotrophia congenita   _____

25. Cleft nose   _____

Conditions of the Perinatal Period - I (760-779)

2003 ICD-9-CM

This unit covers conditions of the perinatal period and may involve both the mother and fetus or infant.

Caution: Item 16 on the next page may be easier to find using the Tabular List.

Using the Tabular List only, identify the three-digit category for:

1. Maternal death _____

2. Prematurity hyperbilirubinemia _____

3. Exceptionally large baby _____

4. Newborn thrush _____

5. Small for dates _____

6. Newborn seizures _____

7. Fractured clavicle from birthing _____

8. Fetal death from labor anoxia _____

9. "Infant of diabetic mother" syndrome _____

10. Placenta previa _____

Conditions of the Perinatal Period - II (760-779)

Using the alphabetic and/or tabular reference, locate the following diseases and code to acceptable specificity, three, four, or five characters.

1. Umbilical cord necrosis _____

2. Petechiae of newborn infant _____

3. Fetal listeriosis _____

4. Accidental birth _____

5. Newborn transitory tachypnea _____

6. Premature delivery of 730 gm. infant _____

7. Drug dependence affecting newborn _____

8. Facial nerve injury of newborn _____

9. Prolonged labor affecting fetus _____

10. Fetal death from pregnancy termination _____

11. Hyaline membrane disease _____

12. Newborn delay in meconium passage _____

13. Fetal alcohol syndrome _____

14. Unstable lie during pregnancy _____

15. ABO erythroblastosis _____

16. Fetal chignon _____

17. Stillborn _____

18. Congenital hydrocele _____

19. Poor fetal growth _____

20. Hydrops fetalis _____

21. Mild newborn asphyxia _____

22. Fetal blood loss from cord hemorrhage _____

23. Newborn hepatitis _____

24. Premature infant anemia _____

25. Exchange transfusion thrombocytopenia _____

Symptoms, Signs and Ill-Defined Conditions - I (780-799)

2003 ICD-9-CM

This section contains codes useful to almost every practice. When you don't know what else to call it, look at coding the symptoms or the signs of the illness or injury that brought the patient to the office.

Using the Tabular List only, identify the three-digit category for:

1. Cardiorespiratory failure _____
2. Hoarseness _____
3. Anorexia _____
4. Old age _____
5. Cardiogenic shock _____
6. Abnormal EEG _____
7. Apnea _____
8. Carpopedal spasm _____
9. Waterbrash _____
10. Abdominal cramps _____

Symptoms, Signs and Ill-Defined Conditions - II (780-799)

Using the alphabetic and/or tabular references, locate the following diseases and code to acceptable specificity, three, four, or five characters.

1. Occult blood in feces _____

2. Headache _____

3. Sudden infant death syndrome (SIDS) _____

4. Transient hypotension _____

5. Belching _____

6. Intermittent staggering gait _____

7. Heart pain _____

8. Male stress and urge incontinence _____

9. Acetone in urine _____

10. Found dead _____

11. Abnormal blushing _____

12. Swollen glands _____

13. Excessive weight gain _____

14. Abnormal weight loss _____

15. Positive TB test _____

16. Nervous tension _____

17. Vertigo _____

18. Enlarged spleen _____

19. Urinary retention _____

20. Coma _____

21. Halitosis _____

22. Coin lesion, left lung _____

23. All worn out _____

24. Abnormal liver scan _____

25. Dropsy _____

Injury and Poisoning - I (800-999)

2003 ICD-9-CM

This unit contains the diagnoses for fractures, dislocations, sprains, wounds, contusions, burns, poisonings, and other toxic effects and complications. Poisonings are easy to find using the Table of Drugs and Chemicals at the end of the Alphabetic Index.

Caution: Watch out (again) for the codes requiring a 5th digit. Also, what kind of injury would result from the incident in item 22 on the next page? Search on that term.

Using the Tabular List only, identify the three-digit category for:

1. Penicillin poisoning _____

2. Anaphylactic shock _____

3. Wrist sprain _____

4. Frostbite _____

5. Fracture temporal bone _____

6. Open wound of toe _____

7. Mechanical complication of dialysis shunt _____

8. Burn of fingers _____

9. Elbow dislocation _____

10. Infected blister _____

Injury and Poisoning - II (800-999)

Using the alphabetic and/or tabular references, locate the following diseases and code to acceptable specificity, three, four, or five characters.

1. Air embolus following transfusion _____

2. C5-C7 cord injury with complete lesion _____

3. Open wound of scalp _____

4. Concussion, in coma after 48 hours _____

5. Open dislocation, acromioclavicular joint _____

6. Sunstroke _____

7. Battered spouse syndrome _____

8. Laceration and chemical burn, lower arm _____

9. Lead oxide paint poisoning _____

10. Peritonitis due to retained surgical sponge _____

11. 3rd degree burn, upper back _____

12. Dropped heavy trunk on left great toe _____

13. 15 infected mosquito bites _____

14. Struck by lightening while golfing _____

15. Open fracture of metatarsal bones _____

16. Rejection of kidney transplant _____

17. Leaking silicone breast implant _____

18. Abrasion, left leg _____

19. Starvation _____

20. Death by drowning _____

21. Open fracture of the sternum _____

22. Esophageal burns, drank "Easy-Off" oven cleaner _____

23. Sprained ankle _____

24. Pneumothorax from stab wound to chest _____

25. Removed 3 small stones from left ear canal _____

Supplementary Classification - "V" Codes - I (V01-V83)

2003 ICD-9-CM

These codes are used as a "diagnosis" for a person who: (a) is receiving services for a specific purpose but is not currently sick, such as vaccination; (b) seeks treatment for a specific disorder such as chemotherapy; or (c) has some circumstance or problem present that influences the patient's health status but is not itself a current illness or injury, such as a history of cancer. Insurers may not pay for many of these codes as they may question the medical necessity of treatment for well persons. Many HMOs providing preventive care expect the office to use these codes when the patient is seen for routine care.

Caution: Some terms are not easy to find in the Alphabetic Index.

Using the Tabular List only, identify the V and two-digit category for:

1. Infant screened for chromosomal anomalies   _____
2. Artificial eye fitting   _____
3. Family planning   _____
4. Measles screening   _____
5. Triplets   _____
6. Seen for ear piercing   _____
7. MMR Immunization   _____
8. Mother died of breast CA   _____
9. Exposure to hepatitis   _____
10. Patient "worried well"   _____

Supplementary Classification - "V" Codes - II (V01-V83)

Using the alphabetic and/or tabular references, locate the following diseases and code to acceptable specificity, three, four, or five characters.

1. Counseling, contraceptive foam use   _____
2. Camp physical exam   _____
3. Twin delivery, 1 stillborn   _____
4. Male, family history of breast CA   _____
5. Adult, was battered as a child   _____
6. Drug allergy by history   _____
7. Cornea donor   _____
8. Going to India, needs cholera vaccine   _____
9. Check status of cystostomy   _____
10. Spent night with syphilitic partner   _____
11. Refugee exam   _____
12. Viral hepatitis carrier   _____
13. Drunk driving test   _____
14. Treated for alcoholism, 1986   _____
15. Routine chest x-ray, food handler   _____
16. Problems with mother-in-law   _____
17. Orthodontia patient   _____
18. Receiving estrogen, postmenopausal   _____
19. Annual Pap smear exam   _____
20. Respirator dependent   _____
21. Recently in India, worried about exposure to cholera   _____
22. Allergy testing   _____
23. Diabetic lifestyle education   _____
24. Screening for sickle-cell disorder   _____
25. C-section delivery of stillborn sextuplets   _____

Supplementary Classification - "E" Codes - I (E800-E999)

2003 ICD-9-CM

These codes describe the external causes of injury or poisoning. They would be used in addition to the actual condition treated. If you set a fractured femur caused by an automobile accident, code the fracture first (primary) and the E code second. The use of the E code could indicate that the primary responsibility for payment rests with some other agency beside the health insurance carrier, such as a taxicab company or the railroad.

Caution: Read the instructions carefully before beginning the coding exercises. Note that the reference to the fourth digit results in a five-character code.

Using the Tabular List only, identify the E and three-digit category for:

1. Train collided with downed tree _____
2. Wood alcohol poisoning _____
3. Fell from ski-lift gondola _____
4. Cigarette burn _____
5. Accidental aspirin poisoning _____
6. Fell out of bed _____
7. Injured by letter bomb _____
8. Accidentally pushed from moving car _____
9. Trampled by crowd in a panic _____
10. Radiation therapy overdose _____

Supplementary Classification - "E" Codes - II (E800-E999)

Using the alphabetic and/or tabular references, locate the following diseases and code to acceptable specificity, three, four, or five characters.

1. Sea anemone sting   _____

2. Passenger hurt when snowmobile hit tree   _____

3. Killed by handgun, possible homicide   _____

4. Bicyclist injured by train   _____

5. Bicyclist collided with wall   _____

6. Slashed wrists in suicide attempt   _____

7. Loss of hearing from rock music   _____

8. Injured during earthquake   _____

9. Diving accident, hit bottom of pool   _____

10. Hurt at camp site, motor home steps collapsed   _____

11. Thrown from horse & buggy in collision with car   _____

12. Injured when hot air balloon crashed   _____

13. 4 y/o drank gasoline from pop bottle   _____

14. Injured by fireworks   _____

15. Overcome by Agent Orange in Viet Nam   _____

16. Failure of aortic valve prosthesis, 4 days post-op   _____

17. Severe reaction, used prescribed dose of eye meds   _____

18. Burned while tending fireplace at cottage   _____

19. Dehydration, water to home turned off   _____

20. Human bites, left arm, 3 y/o male   _____

21. Drowned when washed overboard during storm   _____

22. Infection, contaminated during heart cath   _____

23. Hand slashed by circular saw   _____

24. Accidental ether poisoning at fraternity party   _____

25. Skin frozen, contact with dry ice   _____

Exam Questions for CPT-4, CPT-4 and HCPCS, and ICD-9-CM

Directions:

- Use the appropriate coding manual to determine the correct choice for each situation.
- Answer sheet is provided at the end of each exam for recording your choice for each question.

Exam Questions: CPT–4

1. Patient underwent nerve grafting of the right foot, 3 cm.

   ① 64885

   ② 64890

   ③ 64891

   ④ 64901

2. Patient underwent thyroidectomy for removal of remaining thyroid tissue after previous right lobectomy for suspected malignancy.

   ① 60225

   ② 60240

   ③ 60260

   ④ 60270

3. Established nursing facility resident was seen for annual assessment.

   ① 99201

   ② 99301

   ③ 99302

   ④ 99331

4. An 81-year-old patient receives anesthesia prior to undergoing cardioversion for persistent arrhythmia. Include physical status modifier with code.

   ① 00400-P2 + 99100

   ② 00410-P2

   ③ 00410-P2 + 99100

   ④ 00410-P4

5. Surgeon performs sinusotomy for removal of polyps, including biopsy.

   ① 31020

   ② 31050

   ③ 31051

   ④ 31070

6. Physician performs surgical biopsy of the right temporal artery.

   ① 37605

   ② 37609

   ③ 37799

   ④ 75970

7. A 67-year-old patient underwent contact laser vaporization of the prostate.

   ① 52450

   ② 52601

   ③ 52647

   ④ 52648

8. Patient underwent total abdominal hysterectomy, sparing the tubes and ovaries.

   ① 58150

   ② 58152

   ③ 58200

   ④ 58210

9. Radiologist directs and interprets the placement of a percutaneous gastrostomy tube in a patient who is status post cerebrovascular accident.

   ① 43750

   ② 74340

   ③ 74350

   ④ 74355

10. Nursing home patient was admitted for management of pneumonia which is now resolved. The physician came by the facility to discharge the patient to home, spending 20 minutes with the patient and family.

    ① 99313

    ② 99315

    ③ 99316

    ④ 99321

11. The physician conducted an initial office consultation for a 44-year-old patient, 6 years status post lumbar laminectomy, with intractable sciatic pain, depression, and history of narcotic dependency/abuse, high complexity.

① 99241

② 99243

③ 99244

④ 99245

12. A 16-year-old patient undergoes excision of an aneurysmal bone cyst of the proximal right humerus, with allograft.

① 23155

② 23156

③ 23184

④ 23220

13. A 15-year-old, otherwise healthy patient receives anesthesia for electroconvulsive therapy. Include physical status modifier with code.

① 00104-P1

② 00104-P2

③ 00190-P1

④ 00190-P2

14. Patient who is status post cochlear implant has visit for aural rehabilitation and speech processor programming.

① 92506

② 92507

③ 92510

④ 92557

15. Healthcare employee receives first Hepatitis B vaccination, intramuscular injection.

① 90371

② 90746

③ 90746 + 90782

④ 90746 + 90788

16. Patient underwent cervical conization with loop electrical excision of the transitional zone.

① 57460

② 57500

③ 57520

④ 57522

17. Patient underwent stereotactic biopsy of intracranial lesion under MR guidance.

① 61720

② 61750

③ 61751

④ 61770

18. Dr. Harris counsels a group of at-risk teenagers regarding sexually transmitted diseases and prevention. Session lasts 30 minutes.

① 99401

② 99402

③ 99411

④ 99411-21

19. Dr. Nuri examines an 18-year-old patient in the emergency department for recurrent, severe menstrual migraine headache.

① 99241

② 99281

③ 99282

④ 99284

20. Patient underwent in-office simple incision and drainage of a pilonidal cyst.

① 10060

② 10061

③ 10080

④ 10081

21. Surgeon performs removal of Harrington rod in a patient suffering from chronic irritation in the region of insertion.

① 22849

② 22850

③ 22852

④ 22899

22. Patient with congenital cleft palate underwent rhinoplasty with columellar lengthening, including the septum and tip.

① 30410

② 30430

③ 30460

④ 30462

23. Patient with suspected apnea underwent sleep study with recording of ventilation, respiratory effort, heart rate, and oxygen saturation. Technologist was in attendance.

① 95805

② 95806

③ 95807

④ 95811

24. Surgeon performed excision of pterygium with grafting, left eye.

① 65420

② 65426

③ 67800

④ 67808

25. The neonatologist was asked to be on standby for 25 minutes for cesarean delivery of baby in distress.

① 99360

② 99360-22

③ 99436

④ 99440

26. Physician performed complex repair of a 3.2-cm scalp laceration.

① 13120

② 13120 + 13122

③ 13121

④ 13121 + 13122

27. A 65-year-old patient receives anesthesia for repair of inguinal hernia. The patient has controlled hypertension. Include physical status modifier with code.

① 00830-P1

② 00830-P2

③ 00832-P1

④ 00832-P2

28. The patient underwent creation of burr holes of the skull with evacuation of subdural hematoma.

① 61105

② 61140

③ 61154

④ 61156

29. Five-year-old patient, status post eardrum rupture, undergoes tympanic membrane repair with patch.

① 69433

② 69610

③ 69620

④ 69631

30. The physician calls the patient to discuss confirmatory pathology report regarding the patient's new diagnosis of prostate cancer. The physician discusses transferring the patient's care to an oncologist. The call is considered intermediate in urgency and length.

① 99361

② 99371

③ 99372

④ 99373

31. Anesthesia was administered to patient for gastric bypass procedure performed due to patient's morbid obesity. Include physical status modifier with code.

① 00700-P3

② 00790-P2

③ 00790-P3

④ 00797-P3

32. Physician performed excision of inguinal hidradenitis with complex repair.

① 11450

② 11451

③ 11462

④ 11463

33. Patient was scheduled to undergo extensive internal and external hemorrhoidectomy with fistulectomy. Ten minutes prior to the start of the procedure, after anesthesia had been administered, the patient experienced a rapid decrease in heart rate and the physician canceled the procedure.

① No code should be assigned.

② 46260

③ 46260-52

④ 46260-53

34. Patient underwent cystourethroscopy for laser ablation of two bladder tumors, each approximately 2.7 cm in size.

① 52000

② 52204

③ 52234

④ 52235

35. Patient underwent excision of Peyronie plaque, 4.0 cm, with graft.

① 54060

② 54065

③ 54110

④ 54111

36. Hand specialist performs neuroplasty of the ulnar nerve of the left wrist.

① 64702

② 64704

③ 64719

④ 64721

37. Patient, age 15, is seen by his new doctor for comprehensive medicine/physical examination to include immunizations. Patient also has moderate acne on face and chest.

① 99381

② 99381-25

③ 99384

④ 99384-25

38. Patient underwent replantation of thumb after complete amputation from the distal tip to the MP joint.

① 20816

② 20822

③ 20824

④ 20827

39. Patient underwent operative laryngoscopy for removal of chicken bone fragment.

① 31511

② 31525

③ 31530

④ 31531

40. Patient with history of hypertriglyceridemia but with normal cholesterol levels has triglyceride level drawn.

① 82465

② 83718

③ 84478

④ 84487

41. Asthma patient receives initial evaluation for IPPB treatment.
    ① 94620
    ② 94640
    ③ 94656
    ④ 94660

42. Dr. Ladwig performs independent medical examination for patient Mr. Smith to determine Worker's Compensation impairment rating.
    ① 99450
    ② 99455
    ③ 99456
    ④ 99499

43. Patient receives anesthesia for extracorporeal shock wave lithotripsy with water bath. Patient has mild asthma. Include physical status modifier with code.
    ① 00872-P1
    ② 00872-P2
    ③ 00873-P1
    ④ 00873-P2

44. Patient underwent single-lung transplant with cardiopulmonary bypass employed during the procedure.
    ① 32851
    ② 32852
    ③ 32853
    ④ 32854

45. Patient with intestinal intussusception undergoes reduction through laparotomy approach.
    ① 44005
    ② 44020
    ③ 44050
    ④ 44055

46. Surgeon performs gastric bypass procedure for patient's morbid obesity with small intestine reconstruction to limit absorption.
    ① 43842
    ② 43846
    ③ 43847
    ④ 43848

47. Ms. Jones was seen in an initial office orthopedic consultation for bilateral trochanteric bursitis; visit was considered problem-focused only.
    ① 99241
    ② 99242
    ③ 99245
    ④ 99251

48. Surgeon performs repair of abdominal aortic aneurysm, caused by high-grade atherosclerosis.
    ① 35001
    ② 35081
    ③ 35082
    ④ 35091

49. Dr. Kelly successfully performs resuscitation on an infant with cardiac distress during delivery.
    ① 99432
    ② 99435
    ③ 99436
    ④ 99440

50. Patient underwent excision of 1.5-cm malignant skin lesion of the left calf, as well as removal of Norplant contraceptive capsules.
    ① 11602 + 11976
    ② 11602 + 11976-51
    ③ 11976 + 11602
    ④ 11976 + 11602-51

51. Patient was seen in the office for trigger point injection involving the trapezius and latissimus muscle groups.

① 20551

② 20552

③ 64613

④ 64614

52. Patient underwent hepatic artery ligation with complex suture repair of a liver laceration following motor vehicle accident.

① 47350

② 47360

③ 47360-51

④ 47361

53. Hospital follow-up visit by Dr. Stephens to see a 59-year-old female patient, status post uncomplicated left hip fixation.

① 99221

② 99223

③ 99231

④ 99232

54. Family practitioner performed excision of a lipoma of the right forearm, 1.5 cm in diameter.

① 11402

② 11402 + 12031

③ 11422

④ 11422 + 12031

55. Donor undergoes bone marrow harvesting for transplantation.

① 38220

② 38230

③ 38240

④ 38241

56. Patient underwent total gastrectomy with Roux-en-Y reconstruction for stomach carcinoma.

① 43620

② 43621

③ 43631

④ 43633

57. Surgeon performed simple Burch urethropexy on 45-year-old, mentally underdeveloped female.

① 51800

② 51840

③ 51841

④ 51992

58. Newly diagnosed testicular cancer patient underwent radical orchiectomy with abdominal exploration via inguinal approach.

① 54520

② 54522

③ 54530

④ 54535

59. Patient underwent reconstruction of the mandibular rami due to blunt trauma, undergoing C osteotomy with bone graft.

① 21188

② 21193

③ 21194

④ 21195

60. Patient underwent bilateral angiography of the carotid arteries under direct radiologic supervision.

① 75665

② 75671

③ 75676

④ 75680

61. The patient was seen on initial endocrinology office visit, having been referred for signs and symptoms of new-onset diabetes.

① 99201

② 99204

③ 99212

④ 99214

62. Patient underwent emergency laparoscopic appendectomy.

① 44950

② 44960

③ 44970

④ 44979

63. Patient underwent nephrolithotomy for removal of large staghorn calculus occupying renal pelvis and calyces.

① 50010

② 50065

③ 50075

④ 50081

64. Patient underwent flexible sigmoidoscopy to 60 cm with removal of two small polyps using snare technique.

① 44361

② 44364

③ 44389

④ 44393

65. Dr. Roberts conducts a home visit for a nonambulatory patient with progessing multiple sclerosis, now experiencing respiratory difficulty. The physician spent a total of 45 minutes with the new patient and family discussing treatment options and possible admission to nursing facility.

① 99342

② 99343

③ 99347

④ 99349

66. Surgeon performed limited thoracotomy for lung biopsy.

① 32020

② 32035

③ 32095

④ 32100

67. Patient underwent marsupialization of Bartholin gland cyst.

① 10040

② 10060

③ 56420

④ 56440

68. Patient receives 15 minutes of ultrasound therapy to the left hip for bursitis.

① 97033

② 97035

③ 97110

④ 97124

69. Patient with symptoms of poisoning underwent screening for the presence of arsenic.

① 82157

② 82175

③ 83015

④ 83018

70. Patient underwent pericardial window creation for drainage of excess pericardial fluid.

① 33010

② 33015

③ 33020

④ 33025

71. Patient with simple papilloma of the penis undergoes cryosurgery procedure for removal.

① 54056

② 54057

③ 54065

④ 54110

72. Pain specialist physician performs single lumbar epidural steroid injection.

   ① 62280

   ② 62282

   ③ 62311

   ④ 62318

73. Patient underwent emergency noncontrast head CT scan following blunt trauma to the skull.

   ① 70450

   ② 70470

   ③ 70486

   ④ 70540

74. Nuclear medicine ventilation and perfusion lung scan was performed on patient with sudden shortness of breath; aerosol technique was used, two projections were obtained.

   ① 78584

   ② 78587

   ③ 78588

   ④ 78594

75. Patient was treated with aortofemoral-popliteal bypass grafting for severe occlusive disease.

   ① 35456

   ② 35546

   ③ 35551

   ④ 35651

76. A 12-year-old female patient underwent dilation of the urethra under general anesthesia.

   ① 53605

   ② 53660

   ③ 53661

   ④ 53665

77. Patient underwent radial keratotomy procedure in the right eye.

   ① 65710

   ② 65760

   ③ 65767

   ④ 65771

78. Combative patient underwent removal of burrowed insect from external auditory canal; general anesthesia required.

   ① 69145

   ② 69200

   ③ 69205

   ④ 69220

79. Expectant mother of twins underwent complete obstetrical ultrasound in second trimester.

   ① 76805 + 76810

   ② 76811 + 76812

   ③ 76815

   ④ 76856

80. Patient Young, on parole, was to undergo his first monthly drug testing for marijuana. The lab ran a test to detect the patient's THC level. Two-phase procedure was performed.

   ① 80100

   ② 80100 + 80102

   ③ 80102 quantity 2

   ④ 80103

81. Steelworker was examined in the emergency room with acute eye pain associated with probable steel shaving in the affected eye.

   ① 99281

   ② 99283

   ③ 99284

   ④ 99285

82. Surgeon performs closure of rectovaginal fistula by vaginal approach.

① 57284

② 57300

③ 57305

④ 57310

83. Patient underwent pre- and post-contrast MRI studies of the pelvis.

① 72191

② 72193

③ 72197

④ 72198

84. Surgeon performed open repair of a femoral neck fracture with internal fixation.

① 27230

② 27235

③ 27236

④ 27244

85. Patient underwent tubal ligation with use of Falope rings, vaginal approach.

① 58600

② 58615

③ 58671

④ 58700

86. Patient receives chiropractic manipulative treatment for pain in the temporomandibular joint region.

① 97140

② 98925

③ 98940

④ 98943

87. Patient undergoes sex-change operation, from male to female.

① 55890

② 55899

③ 55970

④ 55980

88. Surgeon performed cesarean delivery after failed VBAC attempt.

① 59514

② 59610

③ 59612

④ 59620

89. Patient underwent cataract extraction with insertion of intraocular lens via phacoemulsification technique.

① 66830

② 66850

③ 66982

④ 66984

Answers to Exam Questions: CPT–4

1. ① ② ③ ④	24. ① ② ③ ④	47. ① ② ③ ④	70. ① ② ③ ④
2. ① ② ③ ④	25. ① ② ③ ④	48. ① ② ③ ④	71. ① ② ③ ④
3. ① ② ③ ④	26. ① ② ③ ④	49. ① ② ③ ④	72. ① ② ③ ④
4. ① ② ③ ④	27. ① ② ③ ④	50. ① ② ③ ④	73. ① ② ③ ④
5. ① ② ③ ④	28. ① ② ③ ④	51. ① ② ③ ④	74. ① ② ③ ④
6. ① ② ③ ④	29. ① ② ③ ④	52. ① ② ③ ④	75. ① ② ③ ④
7. ① ② ③ ④	30. ① ② ③ ④	53. ① ② ③ ④	76. ① ② ③ ④
8. ① ② ③ ④	31. ① ② ③ ④	54. ① ② ③ ④	77. ① ② ③ ④
9. ① ② ③ ④	32. ① ② ③ ④	55. ① ② ③ ④	78. ① ② ③ ④
10. ① ② ③ ④	33. ① ② ③ ④	56. ① ② ③ ④	79. ① ② ③ ④
11. ① ② ③ ④	34. ① ② ③ ④	57. ① ② ③ ④	80. ① ② ③ ④
12. ① ② ③ ④	35. ① ② ③ ④	58. ① ② ③ ④	81. ① ② ③ ④
13. ① ② ③ ④	36. ① ② ③ ④	59. ① ② ③ ④	82. ① ② ③ ④
14. ① ② ③ ④	37. ① ② ③ ④	60. ① ② ③ ④	83. ① ② ③ ④
15. ① ② ③ ④	38. ① ② ③ ④	61. ① ② ③ ④	84. ① ② ③ ④
16. ① ② ③ ④	39. ① ② ③ ④	62. ① ② ③ ④	85. ① ② ③ ④
17. ① ② ③ ④	40. ① ② ③ ④	63. ① ② ③ ④	86. ① ② ③ ④
18. ① ② ③ ④	41. ① ② ③ ④	64. ① ② ③ ④	87. ① ② ③ ④
19. ① ② ③ ④	42. ① ② ③ ④	65. ① ② ③ ④	88. ① ② ③ ④
20. ① ② ③ ④	43. ① ② ③ ④	66. ① ② ③ ④	89. ① ② ③ ④
21. ① ② ③ ④	44. ① ② ③ ④	67. ① ② ③ ④	
22. ① ② ③ ④	45. ① ② ③ ④	68. ① ② ③ ④	
23. ① ② ③ ④	46. ① ② ③ ④	69. ① ② ③ ④	

Exam Questions: CPT-4 and HCPCS

1. If a physician orders ambulance services for a Medicare patient, which modifier applies?

   ① -QM

   ② -QN

   ③ -RC

   ④ -RT

2. A patient underwent simple incision and drainage of an abscess on his thigh. The wound was packed with iodoform gauze (approximately 2 x 2). Select the correct codes for the procedure and the gauze.

   ① 10060 + A6220

   ② 10060 + A6222

   ③ 10061 + A6222

   ④ 10061 + A6223

3. HCPCS Level II codes are four-position alphanumeric codes used to represent items not represented in Level I (CPT) codes.

   ① true

   ② false

4. A patient is to undergo an IVP but has a severe reaction to the contrast material and the IVP procedure is discontinued. Which modifier is used to describe this situation?

   ① -22

   ② -52

   ③ -53

   ④ -56

5. A Medicaid patient was seen in the urgent care center with signs and symptoms of dehydration. She was observed for 8 hours while receiving IV normal saline infusion, 1000 cc. Select the correct HCPCS code.

   ① J7030

   ② J7040

   ③ J7050

   ④ J7120

6. The L group of codes represents which procedures/products?

   ① pathology and laboratory

   ② drugs and enterals

   ③ orthotics and prosthetics

   ④ speech and language services

7. In CPT coding, the history, examination, and medical decision making are considered the key components in selecting the level of E/M services.

   ① true

   ② false

8. If a patient has trigger thumb release performed on the right, which modifier is used to further specify the anatomic location?

   ① -F4

   ② -F5

   ③ -F9

   ④ -FA

9. A nursing facility patient developed multiple decubitus ulcers after a hospital stay. Her physician readmitted her to the nursing facility, developed a new plan of care, and ordered an air fluidized bed for treatment. Select the correct E/M code and the correct HCPCS code.

   ① 99301 + E0193

   ② 99301 + E0194

   ③ 99302 + E0193

   ④ 99302 + E0194

10. The use of HCPCS codes is mandatory on all Medicare and Medicaid claims submitted for payment for services of allied health care professionals.

    ① true

    ② false

11. A patient was seen in consultation for possible surgery. The surgeon schedules the procedure for the following day. Which modifier would you choose to indicate the decision for surgery?

① -54

② -55

③ -56

④ -57

12. Select the correct HCPCS code for an insertion tray without drainage bag or catheter.

① A4310

② A4311

③ A4312

④ A4313

13. Select the correct HCPCS code for surgical stockings, below-knee length.

① A4490

② A4495

③ A4500

④ A4510

14. In CPT coding, the definition of outpatient services would be those provided to a person who only stays in the hospital overnight.

① true

② false

15. A patient has incision and drainage of an abscess involving the left fourth toe. Identify the correct modifier.

① -T2

② -T3

③ -T6

④ -T8

16. The patient was seen in the office for a facial chemical peel, epidermal only.

① 15780

② 15786

③ 15788

④ 15789

17. K codes in HCPCS represent official codes for durable medical equipment.

① true

② false

18. The patient was seen in the emergency department for acute shortness of breath. During his observation in the emergency department, multiple testing of his arterial blood gases was performed to monitor his improvement. Which modifier would you choose to accurately code the multiple ABGs?

① -51

② -90

③ -91

④ -99

19. Select the correct HCPCS code for a tourniquet for a dialysis patient.

① A4911

② A4913

③ A4918

④ A4929

20. Select the correct HCPCS code for a pair of aluminum underarm crutches.

① E0110

② E0112

③ E0114

④ E0116

21. Physical status modifiers in CPT are used to distinguish the varying levels of complexity of surgical services provided.

① true

② false

22. A Medicare patient has been prescribed a wheelchair, but the beneficiary has not decided on whether to purchase or rent. Which HCPCS modifier would you use?

① -BO

② -BP

③ -BR

④ -BU

23. A teenage patient, new to the clinic, was seen for signs and symptoms of tonsillitis and pharyngitis. She was given an injection of azithromycin for her acute symptoms. Select the correct E/M code and the HCPCS code.

① 99201 + J0456

② 99201 + J0530

③ 99202 + J0456

④ 99202 + J0530

24. It is acceptable to code HCPCS from index entries only.

① true

② false

25. A patient was seen by her family doctor for a routine physical exam. During the exam, the patient was noted to have high blood pressure. The physician discussed the new finding with the patient, and the patient disclosed she has been under a great deal of stress due to the demands of her work and impending divorce. The high blood pressure was deemed stress-related and the physician and the patient discussed stress-reduction techniques. As a result of the extended discussion with the patient, the visit was prolonged beyond the normally expected length for a routine physical exam. Which CPT modifier would you use to document the additional time spent with the patient?

① -21

② -22

③ -24

④ -25

26. Select the correct HCPCS code for a surgically implanted electrical osteogenesis stimulator.

① E0748

② E0749

③ E0756

④ E0760

27. Select the correct HCPCS code to represent a patient receiving an injection of amphotericin B, 50 mg.

① J0285

② J0287

③ J0288

④ J0289

28. The general definition of the CPT surgical package includes the patient's preoperative evaluation, the surgical procedure and its usual components, and the patient's uncomplicated follow-up care.

① true

② false

29. The patient has a skin tag removed from her upper left eyelid. Which HCPCS modifier describes this location?

① -E1

② -E2

③ -E3

④ -E4

30. An infant born with clubfoot on the right was seen in the pediatric orthopedic clinic as a new patient. The physician conducted a problem-focused history and examination and prescribed a clubfoot wedge for the patient. Select the correct codes for the visit and the wedge.

① 99201 + L3201

② 99201 + L3380

③ 99212 + L3201

④ 99212 + L3380

31. The HCPCS route of administration abbreviation "IT" means the patient is receiving the drug intrathecally.

① true

② false

32. The patient was seen in the office for exercise stress testing. When the physician was placing the EKG leads, she noticed a suspicious mole on the patient's chest and excised the lesion. What CPT modifier would you use to indicate the additional procedure performed during this visit?

① -50

② -51

③ -52

④ -53

33. A patient was seen in the office for an acute case of hives. The doctor gave her a 25 mg injection of hydroxyzine. Select the correct HCPCS code.

① J3400

② J3410

③ J3470

④ J3485

34. Select the correct HCPCS code for an orthopedic shoe insole made of felt and covered with leather.

① L3520

② L3540

③ L3570

④ L3590

35. To measure and code the removal of a lesion using CPT guidelines, the lesion size must be expressed in inches.

① true

② false

36. If a patient is prescribed oxygen therapy at 0.5 liters per minute, which HCPCS modifier would you choose to describe this flow rate?

① -QE

② -QF

③ -QG

④ -QH

37. An established patient was seen in the office because of difficulty toileting after hip replacement surgery. The physician examined the patient and sent her home with a stationary commode chair with fixed arms to use during her recovery period. Select the appropriate codes.

① 99211 + E0163

② 99211 + E0164

③ 99212 + E0163

④ 99212 + E0164

38. All HCPCS codes and descriptions are updated monthly by CMS.

① true

② false

39. Which CPT modifier would you choose to indicate a patient received a service or procedure that was less than originally intended?

① -22

② -32

③ -51

④ -52

40. Select the correct HCPCS code that describes the reduction of an ocular prosthesis.

① V2623

② V2625

③ V2626

④ V2629

41. A patient was given an intramuscular injection of 2 mg of Haldol in the physician's office. Select the correct HCPCS code.

① J1630

② J1631

③ J3410

④ J3470

42. When coding bilateral procedures in CPT, you must always include the code 09950.

① true

② false

43. The mobile x-ray service came to the nursing facility to x-ray Mrs. Jones for possible hip fracture. The x-ray will be interpreted the following day by the radiologist. Which HCPCS modifier would you use in this circumstance?

① -TA

② -TC

③ -TD

④ -TF

44. A patient was seen in the emergency department for an acute asthma attack. The physician conducted an expanded problem focused history and examination and the patient was given nebulizer treatments of albuterol. Select the correct codes.

① 99281 + J7618

② 99281 + J7619

③ 99282 + J7618

④ 99282 + J7619

45. Laboratory services in HCPCS are listed in the P codes grouping.

① true

② false

46. Which CPT modifier would you use to indicate that an outside laboratory was used to process a patient's specimen?

① -56

② -90

③ -91

④ -99

47. Select the correct HCPCS code for a patient receiving nonemergency transportation in the mountain area via minibus.

① A0080

② A0110

③ A0120

④ A0160

48. Many radiology procedures include two parts: a technical component and a professional component.

① true

② false

49. The patient has been using his wheelchair for nearly four years. Due to wear and tear, he now needs a replacement for the right footrest. Which HCPCS modifier can you use to indicate this replacement?

① -RC

② -RP

③ -RR

④ -RT

50. A patient was referred to the office of a wound care specialist for consultation regarding his nonhealing surgical wound. The physician spent approximately 30 minutes with the patient and sent him home on topical hyperbaric oxygen chamber therapy for wound healing. Select the correct codes.

① 99241 + A4575

② 99242 + A4575

③ 99251 + A4575

④ 99252 + A4575

51. Drugs listed in HCPCS are identified by both brand and generic names.

① true

② false

52. A patient underwent emergency cholecystectomy six days after having undergone a lung biopsy. The same surgeon performed both procedures. Which CPT modifier is used to indicate this type of situation?

① -58

② -59

③ -78

④ -79

53. Which of the following HCPCS code groups are listed for use only on a temporary basis?

① G, J, Q

② K, G, Q

③ K, J, Q

④ Q, P, K

54. A patient was seen for insertion of a temporary indwelling urinary catheter, Foley type. Select the correct HCPCS codes.

① 51701 + A4314

② 51701 + A4338

③ 51702 + A4338

④ 51703 + A4328

55. According to CPT coding guidelines, a pathology consultation is the same as a medical interpretive report.

① true

② false

56. Dr. Wilkins performed amputation of a patient's right lower extremity (BKA). His staff PA was the assistant during the procedure. Which HCPCS modifier would you choose to indicate the PA's role in this procedure?

① -AD

② -AM

③ -AS

④ -AT

57. Patient was seen for routine visit in the multiple sclerosis clinic. The patient received an injection of beta-1a interferon, 33 mcg, by the nurse in the clinic. Select the appropriate codes.

① 99211 + J1825

② 99211 + J1830

③ 99212 + J9212

④ 99212 + J9214

58. HCPCS ambulance modifiers always include one alpha character and one numeric character.

① true

② false

59. If a patient suddenly refuses to have surgery performed after being prepped for the procedure, which CPT modifier would you use to indicate the change in plans?

① -52

② -53

③ -56

④ none of the above

60. Select the correct HCPCS code for a drainable rubber ostomy pouch that has a faceplate attached.

① A4375

② A4376

③ A4377

④ A4378

61. Select the correct HCPCS code for replacement handgrip for a cane that the patient owns.

① A4635

② A4636

③ A4637

④ A4640

62. In CPT coding, when the patient receives an immune globulin product, you must also include an administration code as appropriate.

① true

② false

63. An ambulance was called to come to the aid of a choking patient; however, the patient expired before the ambulance arrived on the scene. Which HCPCS modifier would you use to document this circumstance?

① -QK

② -QL

③ -QM

④ -QP

64. Patient underwent unattended sleep study with monitoring of oxygen saturation. The patient was not able to sleep adequately throughout the study and therefore the study was equivocal. The patient was provided with a recording apnea monitor for home use. Select the appropriate codes.

① 95806 + E0618

② 95806 + E0619

③ 95807 + E0618

④ 95807 + E0619

65. The three levels of national codes can be applied to both inpatients and outpatients.

① true

② false

66. Which CPT modifier is used to indicate a repeat procedure performed by a different physician?

① -58

② -76

③ -77

④ -78

67. Select the correct HCPCS code for hydrogel dressing with an adhesive border used to cover a wound, measuring 24 square inches.

① A6242

② A6243

③ A6246

④ A6248

68. Select the correct HCPCS code for home mix parenteral nutrition additives, to include electrolytes.

① B4197

② B4199

③ B4216

④ B4220

69. When coding in CPT, no distinction is made between new and established patients in the emergency department.

① true

② false

70. The patient was seen in the contraceptive clinic two weeks after delivery of her child. She was fitted with a copper intrauterine device. Select the codes for the fitting and the device.

① 58300 + A4260

② 58300 + J7300

③ 58301 + A4260

④ 58301 + J7300

71. Select the correct HCPCS code for a brake attachment for wheeled walker.

① E0145
② E0147
③ E0155
④ E0159

72. Select the correct HCPCS code to reflect a patient being admitted as an inpatient to a resident addiction program for acute alcohol detoxification.

① H0009
② H0011
③ H0012
④ H0013

73. A patient was fitted with a TENS unit for pain control after suffering a fractured radius. Select appropriate codes.

① 64550 + E0720
② 64550 + E0730
③ 64575 + E0720
④ 64575 + E0730

74. Select the correct HCPCS code to represent receiving an injection of methylprednisolone acetate, 40 mg.

① J1020
② J1030
③ J1040
④ J1051

75. The patient presented to the office to have her B_{12} level drawn and to subsequently receive her weekly B_{12} shot. Select the correct codes.

① 82607 + J3420
② 82607 + Q3012
③ 82608 + J3420
④ 82608 + Q3012

76. Select the HCPCS code that correctly identifies a unit of leukocyte-reduced platelets.

① P9019
② P9020
③ P9031
④ P9034

77. Select the correct HCPCS code for 1 mg of inhaled dexamethasone in concentrated form.

① J1094
② J1100
③ J7637
④ J7638

78. A patient who is status post left-sided CVA was seen due to weight loss and other symptoms indicative of dysphagia. She underwent dysphagia screening, and subsequently underwent her first treatment for swallowing dysfunction. Select the codes for the dysphagia screening and the treatment.

① 92525 + V5362
② 92525 + V5364
③ 92526 + V5362
④ 92526 + V5364

79. Select the correct HCPCS code for a non-heated humidifier used with a positive airway pressure device.

① A7039
② E0550
③ E0556
④ K0268

80. The physician saw his patient on the day of discharge and spent 30 minutes with the patient and family to discuss discharge plans, as well as the patient's immediate at-home care. The patient had undergone his second below-knee amputation, and was given a transfer board for use at home. Select the codes for the discharge visit and the transfer board.

① 99238 + E0972

② 99238 + E1035

③ 99239 + E0972

④ 99239 + E1035

81. Select the correct HCPCS code that reflects the supply of one vial of technetium Tc 99m disofenin.

① A9500

② A9502

③ A9510

④ A9511

82. Identify the HCPCS code that describes a full-leg, segmental pneumatic appliance with compressor.

① E0650

② E0660

③ E0667

④ E0671

83. Select the HCPCS code that describes a patient receiving a 50 mg intravenous infusion of cisplatin in the physician's office.

① J0743

② J0780

③ J9060

④ J9062

● Answers to Exam Questions: CPT-4 and HCPCS

1. ① ② ③ ④   23. ① ② ③ ④   45. ① ② ③ ④   67. ① ② ③ ④

2. ① ② ③ ④   24. ① ② ③ ④   46. ① ② ③ ④   68. ① ② ③ ④

3. ① ② ③ ④   25. ① ② ③ ④   47. ① ② ③ ④   69. ① ② ③ ④

4. ① ② ③ ④   26. ① ② ③ ④   48. ① ② ③ ④   70. ① ② ③ ④

5. ① ② ③ ④   27. ① ② ③ ④   49. ① ② ③ ④   71. ① ② ③ ④

6. ① ② ③ ④   28. ① ② ③ ④   50. ① ② ③ ④   72. ① ② ③ ④

7. ① ② ③ ④   29. ① ② ③ ④   51. ① ② ③ ④   73. ① ② ③ ④

8. ① ② ③ ④   30. ① ② ③ ④   52. ① ② ③ ④   74. ① ② ③ ④

9. ① ② ③ ④   31. ① ② ③ ④   53. ① ② ③ ④   75. ① ② ③ ④

10. ① ② ③ ④   32. ① ② ③ ④   54. ① ② ③ ④   76. ① ② ③ ④

11. ① ② ③ ④   33. ① ② ③ ④   55. ① ② ③ ④   77. ① ② ③ ④

12. ① ② ③ ④   34. ① ② ③ ④   56. ① ② ③ ④   78. ① ② ③ ④

13. ① ② ③ ④   35. ① ② ③ ④   57. ① ② ③ ④   79. ① ② ③ ④

14. ① ② ③ ④   36. ① ② ③ ④   58. ① ② ③ ④   80. ① ② ③ ④

15. ① ② ③ ④   37. ① ② ③ ④   59. ① ② ③ ④   81. ① ② ③ ④

16. ① ② ③ ④   38. ① ② ③ ④   60. ① ② ③ ④   82. ① ② ③ ④

17. ① ② ③ ④   39. ① ② ③ ④   61. ① ② ③ ④   83. ① ② ③ ④

18. ① ② ③ ④   40. ① ② ③ ④   62. ① ② ③ ④

19. ① ② ③ ④   41. ① ② ③ ④   63. ① ② ③ ④

20. ① ② ③ ④   42. ① ② ③ ④   64. ① ② ③ ④

21. ① ② ③ ④   43. ① ② ③ ④   65. ① ② ③ ④

22. ① ② ③ ④   44. ① ② ③ ④   66. ① ② ③ ④

Exam Questions: ICD-9-CM

1. The patient was seen in the office today. The patient has known Graves disease, now with signs and symptoms of a thyroid storm.

   ① 242.01

   ② 242.20

   ③ 242.9

   ④ 242.91

2. Three-year-old patient was brought in by her mother because of fever, fussiness, and tugging at the right ear. Otoscopy confirmed acute infection of the canal, with erythema and pus of the canal noted on exam.

   ① 380.10

   ② 381.00

   ③ 382.0

   ④ 382.00

3. Patient was seen because of pain and swelling of the right elbow. The joint does not appear to be unstable. Rule out fracture.

   ① 719.02

   ② 719.42 + 719.02

   ③ 812.20

   ④ 812.40

4. Patient was seen today for allergic reaction to ampicillin, with urticaria and swelling. The patient had taken the medication as directed; classic signs of allergic reaction.

   ① 708.0

   ② 708.0 + 995.2

   ③ 708.0 + 995.2 + E930.0

   ④ 708.0 + E930.0

5. Newly diagnosed asthma patient was counseled regarding asthma therapy and the correct use of a nebulizer.

   ① V65.2

   ② V65.40

   ③ V65.49

   ④ V65.8

6. Select the correct code(s) for ulcerative impetigo caused by a superficial staph infection.

   ① 111.9

   ② 684

   ③ 686

   ④ 686.9

7. Patient was seen for evaluation of pilonidal cyst.

   ① 173.5

   ② 685.0

   ③ 685.1

   ④ 686.0

8. Patient came into the clinic for examination of a penile lesion; physician determined it is a classic plaque of Peyronie disease.

   ① 607.89

   ② 607.9

   ③ 608.89

   ④ 709.9

9. Patient was seen for annual gynecological exam including Pap smear.

   ① V70.0

   ② V70.9

   ③ V72.3

   ④ V76.2

10. Select the correct code(s) for patient counseling regarding contraceptive use; patient is new to Norplant contraceptive.

   ① V25.09
   ② V25.40
   ③ V25.43
   ④ V65.40

11. Patient fell while snowboarding, suffering a dislocation of the left shoulder.

   ① 831
   ② 831.00 + E885.4
   ③ 831.09
   ④ 831.19 + E885.4

12. Select the correct code(s) for bilateral, nonstrangulated inguinal hernia.

   ① 550.10
   ② 550.90
   ③ 550.92
   ④ 550.93

13. Patient was seen for vaginal bleeding in twenty-first week of pregnancy.

   ① 623.8
   ② 640.03
   ③ 640.93
   ④ 641.10

14. A 35-year-old female was seen in the office today for evaluation of a breast lump.

   ① 610.10
   ② 611
   ③ 611.2
   ④ 611.72

15. A 16-year-old male was seen in the clinic for severe sore throat, redness, cough, and erythema. Rapid strep test was positive.

   ① 034
   ② 034.0
   ③ 462 + 034.0
   ④ 463

16. Select the correct code(s) for personal history of cervical carcinoma.

   ① 180.9
   ② 239.5
   ③ V10.40
   ④ V10.41

17. Patient was seen for continued treatment of post-traumatic stress disorder.

   ① 309.0
   ② 309.81
   ③ 309.83
   ④ 309.9

18. Patient was diagnosed with bulimia.

   ① 307.50
   ② 307.51
   ③ 783.0
   ④ 783.6

19. Patient was seen with diarrhea, abdominal cramping, and bloody stools. Rule out ulcerative colitis.

   ① 556.9
   ② 556.9 + 578.1 + 787.91
   ③ 578.1 + 787.91 + 789.00
   ④ 787.91

20. Child was seen for treatment of erythema and puncture wounds of the right forearm due to cat bite.

① 880.03

② 881.00

③ 881.00 + E906.3

④ E906.3

21. Patient was seen in the clinic to discuss treatment options for new diagnosis of malignant melanoma of the forehead.

① 172.0

② 172.3

③ 172.8

④ 172.9

22. Infant was brought in for evaluation of skin tags of the outer ear/earlobe.

① 744.1

② 744.29

③ 757.39

④ 757.8

23. Patient's daughter brought the patient in for follow-up of progressive Alzheimer's dementia.

① 294.10

② 294.8

③ 331.0

④ 331.0 + 294.10

24. Child was brought into the office for evaluation and examination after swallowing a dime.

① 933.0

② 934.8

③ 935.2

④ 938

25. Vacationing patient was seen in the urgent care clinic for second-degree burns on bilateral shoulder areas.

① 692.74

② 692.76

③ 692.82

④ 692.89

26. Select the correct code(s) for Lyme disease.

① 083.9

② 088

③ 088.81

④ 088.9

27. Patient came in for an office visit seeking treatment for fungal toenail infection.

① 110.1

② 110.8

③ 681.11

④ 681.9

28. Patient was seen in the office today requesting medications to assist with alcohol withdrawal.

① 291.0

② 291.4

③ 291.81

④ 291.89

29. Patient was seen for follow-up of replantation of amputated long finger.

① 883.0

② 884.0

③ 886.0

④ 886.1

30. A 6-year-old patient was brought in for additional testing for color blindness.

① 368.55

② 368.59

③ 368.60

④ 368.8

31. Patient was evaluated for somnolence relating to reactive hypoglycemia.

    ① 251.1

    ② 251.1 + 780.09

    ③ 251.2 + 780.0

    ④ 251.2 + 780.09

32. Select the correct code(s) for malignant hypertensive heart disease with renal failure.

    ① 401.0 + 593.9

    ② 403.90

    ③ 404.02

    ④ 405.01

33. Patient was seen for preoperative cardio-vascular evaluation prior to undergoing cholecystectomy.

    ① V72.81

    ② V72.83

    ③ V72.85

    ④ V72.9

34. Patient was seen in follow-up for boxer's fracture of the right extremity.

    ① 814.00

    ② 815.00

    ③ 815.09

    ④ 815.10

35. Select the correct code(s) for cellulitis of the colostomy site.

    ① 569.60

    ② 569.61

    ③ 682.2

    ④ 998.59

36. Select the correct code(s) for congenital bowleggedness.

    ① 736.42

    ② 736.5

    ③ 754.4

    ④ 754.44

37. Patient was seen in the gastroenterology clinic for evaluation of prolapsed internal hemorrhoids and anal fissure.

    ① 455.1 + 565.0

    ② 455.2 + 565.0

    ③ 455.7 + 565.1

    ④ 455.8 + 565.0

38. Patient was seen in the office due to severe vertigo and loss of hearing. The patient was diagnosed with viral labyrinthitis.

    ① 386.19

    ② 386.30

    ③ 386.35

    ④ 780.4

39. Select the correct code(s) for idiopathic scoliosis with backache.

    ① 724.5

    ② 737.3

    ③ 737.30 + 724.5

    ④ 737.4

40. Patient was evaluated for varicose veins with stasis dermatitis of the left lower extremity.

    ① 447.2

    ② 451.0

    ③ 453.8

    ④ 454.1

41. Twenty-year-old patient was seen for continued evaluation of Turner syndrome.

    ① 752.7

    ② 758.6

    ③ 758.7

    ④ 758.8

42. Patient was seen with complaints of melena and anemia. Patient has strong family history of stomach cancer.

① 578.1 + 280.0 + V10.04

② 578.1 + 280.0 + V16.0

③ 578.2 + 280.0 + V16.0

④ V16.0

43. Select the correct code(s) for diabetic cataracts.

① 250.50 + 366.41

② 250.50 + 366.9

③ 250.51 + 366.41

④ 250.51 + 366.09

44. Patient was seen in follow-up for right bundle branch block with incomplete left bundle branch block.

① 426.4 + 426.3

② 426.53

③ 426.54

④ 426.7

45. The patient is status post PTCA, in for one-week follow-up visit.

① V45.81

② V45.82

③ V67.00

④ V67.09

46. Patient was seen for complaints of fatigue and was noted to have diffuse adenopathy. Rule out leukemia.

① 208.00

② 208.80

③ 785.6 + 208.00

④ 785.6 + 780.79

47. Patient's chief complaint is that of losing her sense of smell after a bout of the flu.

① 349.9

② 781.1

③ 782.0

④ 799.2

48. Patient was seen for treatment of situational depression due to impending divorce.

① 308.3

② 309.0

③ 309.1

④ 309.24

49. Select the correct code(s) for acquired trigger finger.

① 727.03

② 727.09

③ 756.89

④ 756.9

50. Select the correct code(s) for rupture of the Achilles tendon.

① 726.81

② 727.5

③ 727.6

④ 727.67

51. Patient was seen for vaginal bleeding; placenta previa was detected. Patient is in early second trimester of pregnancy.

① 640.03

② 641.03

③ 641.10

④ 641.13

52. Select the correct code(s) for narcolepsy.

① 301.81

② 307.45

③ 347

④ 780.50

53. Patient had been suffering episodes of "zoning out" and, after extensive observation and testing, was diagnosed with absence seizures.

① 345.00

② 345.01

③ 345.10

④ 345.40

54. Child was found to have a severe allergy to dog hair.

① 477.0

② 477.8

③ 477.9

④ 478.1

55. Patient was seen in the clinic for treatment of frostbite of the toes.

① 991.2

② 991.3

③ 991.4

④ 991.6

56. Patient suffered an accidental, self-inflicted laceration of the palm of his hand while using a kitchen knife.

① 880.03 + E920.3

② 882.0 + E920.3

③ 882.0 + E920.8

④ 882.00 + E920.8

57. Patient was seen in consultation for narcotic addiction (hydrocodone), episodic.

① 304.02

② 304.60

③ 304.62

④ 305.40

58. Patient visiting from out of state was evaluated and treated with headache, nausea, and vomiting. The patient was diagnosed with altitude sickness.

① 787.01

② 787.02

③ 993.2

④ E902.0

59. Select the correct code(s) for acute staphylococcal conjunctivitis.

① 032.81

② 077.4

③ 372.00

④ 372.03

60. Select the correct code(s) for accidental poisoning with whiskey.

① 980.0 + E860.0

② 980.0 + E860.1

③ 980.9

④ 980.9 + E860.0

61. Patient was seen in the office for ongoing evaluation of dysphasia after he suffered a cerebrovascular accident six months prior.

① 438.12

② 438.13

③ 784.49

④ 784.5

62. Select the correct code(s) for metastatic carcinoma of the liver with unknown primary.

① 155.0 + 239.0

② 197.7 + 199.1

③ 197.7 + 155.0

④ 197.7 + 239.0

63. The patient was seen in the clinic for complaint of halitosis.

① 783.9

② 784.49

③ 784.9

④ 787.9

64. Select the correct code(s) for central corneal ulcer probably due to improper contact lens use and care.

① 370.00

② 370.03

③ 370.33

④ 370.49

65. The patient was seen by the orthopedic physician regarding carpal tunnel syndrome.

① 354.0

② 354.8

③ 354.9

④ 354.00

66. The patient suffered a severe burn over one year ago and is being evaluated for continued neuropathy of the left thigh secondary to the burn.

① 353.6 + 906.8

② 355.71 + 906.7

③ 355.8 + 906.7

④ 355.8 + 906.8

67. Patient was seen in the clinic for treatment of pain due to phantom limb syndrome.

① 353.6

② 353.7

③ 353.8

④ 353.9

68. Select the correct code(s) for ateriovenous malformation of the right lower extremity requiring surgical treatment.

① 747.49

② 747.60

③ 747.64

④ 747.89

69. Infant was seen in the office today for follow-up of Tetrology of Fallot.

① 745.2

② 745.4

③ 746.09

④ 746.4

70. Patient is being treated in the clinic for severe mitral regurgitation.

① 394.9

② 396.0

③ 424.0

④ 424.1

71. Patient was seen and treated for laceration and puncture wound of the right nostril; fish hook accidentally embedded in nostril.

① 873.21 + E920.8

② 873.22 + E920.8

③ 873.29 + E920.8

④ 873.32 + E920.8

72. Select the correct code(s) for chronic familial pemphigus.

① 694.4

② 694.61

③ 757.39

④ 785.4

73. Patient is seen in the office for physical therapy to regain strength in his back after injury at work; thoracic muscle strain.

① 847.1 + V57.1

② 847.9 + V57.1

③ V57.1 + 847.1

④ V57.8 + 847.1

74. Select the correct code for temporomandibular joint syndrome (TMJ).

① 524.4

② 524.60

③ 524.9

④ 524.69

75. Patient was seen for evaluation and treatment of neurogenic bladder.

① 596.4

② 596.53

③ 596.54

④ 596.8

76. Patient was seen in the office because of complaints of urinary symptoms. On digital exam, the patient was found to have a multinodular prostate gland.

① 600.0

② 600.1

③ 600.3

④ 600.9

77. The patient was seen today for weekly chemotherapy infusion; recent diagnosis of carcinoma of the descending colon (primary).

① V58.1 + 153.2

② V58.1 + 235.2

③ V66.2 + 135.2

④ V66.2 + 235.2

78. Patient is being seen in treatment of acute reactive depression due to recent diagnosis of pancreatic cancer.

① 289.9 + 239.0

② 300.4 + 157.1

③ 300.4 + 157.9

④ 300.4 + 239.0

79. Select the correct code(s) for sinusitis, acute, in conjunction with influenza.

① 461.9

② 473.8

③ 473.9

④ 487.1

80. Injuries after assault: The patient suffered a periorbital hematoma, nasal bone fracture, and chipped tooth.

① 921.2 + 802.00 + 873.63 + E960.0

② 921.2 + 802.00 + 873.73 + E960.0

③ 921.3 + 802.00 + 873.63 + E960.0

④ 921.9 + 802.00 + 873.63

81. Select the correct code(s) for a hiatal hernia with obstruction.

① 552.3

② 552.9

③ 553.8

④ 750.6

82. Patient complains of insomnia.

① 307.42

② 307.49

③ 780.51

④ 780.52

83. Patient is being evaluated for sudden total blindness of the right eye; left eye was not affected.

    ① 368.60

    ② 369.60

    ③ 369.63

    ④ 369.64

84. Select the correct code(s) for cardiac asthma.

    ① 428.1

    ② 428.11

    ③ 493.20

    ④ 493.90

85. Adult male was diagnosed with whooping cough due to parapertussis.

    ① 033.1

    ② 033.9

    ③ 306.1

    ④ 786.2

86. Patient was suffering from near-syncope episodes and was diagnosed with an electrolyte imbalance.

    ① 276.0

    ② 276.4

    ③ 276.5

    ④ 276.9

87. Patient is positive for HIV and now has evidence of Kaposi lesions on the skin.

    ① 042

    ② 042 + 176.0

    ③ 757.33

    ④ V08

88. Patient has obvious dependent edema; is in third trimester of pregnancy.

    ① 643.80

    ② 646.10

    ③ 646.13

    ④ 646.20

89. The patient has been diagnosed with multiple sclerosis.

    ① 337.9

    ② 340

    ③ 341.8

    ④ 341.9

90. Select the correct code(s) for a pathologic fracture of the distal radius.

    ① 733.10

    ② 733.12

    ③ 733.19

    ④ 813.06

● Answers to Exam Questions: ICD-9-CM

1. ① ② ③ ④	24. ① ② ③ ④	47. ① ② ③ ④	70. ① ② ③ ④
2. ① ② ③ ④	25. ① ② ③ ④	48. ① ② ③ ④	71. ① ② ③ ④
3. ① ② ③ ④	26. ① ② ③ ④	49. ① ② ③ ④	72. ① ② ③ ④
4. ① ② ③ ④	27. ① ② ③ ④	50. ① ② ③ ④	73. ① ② ③ ④
5. ① ② ③ ④	28. ① ② ③ ④	51. ① ② ③ ④	74. ① ② ③ ④
6. ① ② ③ ④	29. ① ② ③ ④	52. ① ② ③ ④	75. ① ② ③ ④
7. ① ② ③ ④	30. ① ② ③ ④	53. ① ② ③ ④	76. ① ② ③ ④
8. ① ② ③ ④	31. ① ② ③ ④	54. ① ② ③ ④	77. ① ② ③ ④
9. ① ② ③ ④	32. ① ② ③ ④	55. ① ② ③ ④	78. ① ② ③ ④
10. ① ② ③ ④	33. ① ② ③ ④	56. ① ② ③ ④	79. ① ② ③ ④
11. ① ② ③ ④	34. ① ② ③ ④	57. ① ② ③ ④	80. ① ② ③ ④
12. ① ② ③ ④	35. ① ② ③ ④	58. ① ② ③ ④	81. ① ② ③ ④
13. ① ② ③ ④	36. ① ② ③ ④	59. ① ② ③ ④	82. ① ② ③ ④
14. ① ② ③ ④	37. ① ② ③ ④	60. ① ② ③ ④	83. ① ② ③ ④
15. ① ② ③ ④	38. ① ② ③ ④	61. ① ② ③ ④	84. ① ② ③ ④
16. ① ② ③ ④	39. ① ② ③ ④	62. ① ② ③ ④	85. ① ② ③ ④
17. ① ② ③ ④	40. ① ② ③ ④	63. ① ② ③ ④	86. ① ② ③ ④
18. ① ② ③ ④	41. ① ② ③ ④	64. ① ② ③ ④	87. ① ② ③ ④
19. ① ② ③ ④	42. ① ② ③ ④	65. ① ② ③ ④	88. ① ② ③ ④
20. ① ② ③ ④	43. ① ② ③ ④	66. ① ② ③ ④	89. ① ② ③ ④
21. ① ② ③ ④	44. ① ② ③ ④	67. ① ② ③ ④	90. ① ② ③ ④
22. ① ② ③ ④	45. ① ② ③ ④	68. ① ② ③ ④	
23. ① ② ③ ④	46. ① ② ③ ④	69. ① ② ③ ④	